THE EDCORPS CLASSROOM

USING ENTREPRENEURSHIP IN THE
CLASSROOM TO MAKE LEARNING A REAL,
RELEVANT, AND SILO BUSTING EXPERIENCE

CHRIS AVILES

EduMatch Publishing

Published by EduMatch®
PO Box 150324, Alexandria, VA 22315
www.edumatchpublishing.com

These books are available at special discounts when purchased in quantities of 10 or more for use as premiums, promotions fundraising, and educational use. For inquiries and details, contact the publisher: sarah@edumatch.org.

ISBN: 978-1-970133-52-3

To Rachel.

For Oliver. The future is yours.

CONTENTS

Chapter 1

EDCORPS ORIGIN STORIES

So, It Begins

Using entrepreneurship as a vehicle for instruction has been the most rewarding experience of my career. Through all of the successes and failures we've had, there has been significant student learning happening all along the way. Serious, deep learning. The kind that makes you proud to be a teacher. Entrepreneurship empowers students to take ownership of their learning because they know if their business is going to be successful, it is up to them. Students have to use everything they've learned in their other classes — math, art, science, literacy, and every other subject that we teach in silos — in an authentic way. Students are no longer consumers in my class; they're creators and producers. Like our products, my students are shipping their passion and ideas all over the world. Through entrepreneurship, my students have rushed right passed engagement to empowerment because the experiences they are having are real, relevant, and under their control. I should have realized the power of entrepreneurship earlier in my career.

Back when I was teaching high school English, I would assign students a yearlong project called the *Be About It* project. The purpose of the *Be About It* project was to help students find and grow their passions. During the project, over the year, students could pursue something they've always wanted to do. All I asked was that they get up on a stage at the end of the year and tell us what they did, why they did, and what they learned. Many of my students decided to start their own business for the project. Fast forward six years, and entrepreneurship would become my main method of teaching.

FH Gizmos (the FH stands for Fair Haven, our town) was my first, true Education Corporation (EdCorps). Like most businesses, FH Gizmos was born out of the need to solve a problem. When I started working at Knollwood Middle School in Fair Haven, NJ, I was asked to start a makerspace/STEAM class for fifth and sixth graders. I called this class the "Innovation Lab." In the Innovation Lab, we used design thinking to create value for others. My goal was to expose my students to computer science, engineering, and the digital arts through project-based learning (PBL) and, more importantly, gain the experience and attitude they'll need to be successful when they grow up. Six months after launching The Innovation Lab, I realized I had a problem.

Students Lead the Way

One way I expose students to engineering is by having them take apart, analyze, and reassemble unwanted electronics donated by our community. Students love to deconstruct these electronics, see how they work, and then try to reassemble them. The reassembly part usually doesn't go well. Students often struggle to put the electronics back together. I often had full-sized garbage cans of parts piling up in the lab. These parts couldn't be thrown away in the regular trash. They had to be picked up monthly by our school's electronics recycling contractor. I was losing a lot of space in my classroom, and I wasn't happy with the amount of waste we were generating. I could have stopped letting students take apart electronics, but they loved to do it. I had to find a better way.

I asked students how we could limit or eliminate the waste in our class-room. Students came up with an idea we called Parts to Arts. After taking something apart, if students couldn't put it back together, they could upcycle the parts into pieces of art. Like the deconstruction process, my kids loved the Parts to Arts initiative. They were producing tons of art, like circuit board jewelry, wire sculptures, and transistor paintings, but the Parts to Project didn't actually solve the problem. Instead of leftover parts in overflowing trash cans, we now had a bunch of upcycled art projects everywhere. Could we take Parts to Arts to another level?

Again, I asked students: what can we do with all this wonderful artwork? After some brainstorming and collaboration, it was unani-mous: my kids wanted to sell them.

Students decided that having a physical storefront wasn't practical. We'd have to sell our upcycled art online. I have a lot of experience with WordPress, so it didn't take me long to build them an online marketplace. Our marketplace was set up to work like Amazon. Each team of students got a login for the site. Once logged in, students could create their own product page. Once the product page was approved, I linked their product page to the homepage. When customers visited the homepage of our site, they would see all the products students had for sale. When they clicked on a product, it brought them to the student-created product page where they could place an order.

Once the first student-product launched, my classroom was trans-formed. Students began to form teams around ideas they had for prod-ucts they could sell. As they worked together to sell their art, they began to talk about their teams, ideas, and products as if they were running a real business together.

Next thing I knew, students were naming their imaginary businesses. Student product pages evolved into business pages where my kids were now offering entire product lines. These pages had their business' name, colors, and a logo. One page even had a contact form so people could request custom orders or ask questions!

It wasn't long before students asked me if they could sell things other than art. Soon students started to offer all kinds of different products and services. Students were selling products like 3D prints, custom YouTube Artwork, Minecraft skins, and school supplies. One team was even selling custom theme songs for content creators.

The Innovation Lab started to feel like Shark Tank. Students started assigning valuations to their businesses. They were signing contracts that laid out team members' job descriptions and how much equity each student would get in their business. They started to assign themselves roles like Chief Executive Officer and Vice President of Marketing. They created slogans to put on their business cards and got into shouting matches over how much they should sell their products for and whether or not they should offer discounts. They were on fire. In the beginning, I sat back and watched them transform into entrepreneurs, but toward the end of that school year, I did my best to fan the flames.

I told students if we were going to make any sales, we had to buy a domain. To buy a domain, we needed a name. I had them research what makes a good business name and encouraged them to come up with a name that would be special to our school. After a lot of workshopping, we came up with FH Gizmos. FH for Fair Haven, their town, and Gizmos because it was vague enough that they could sell anything they wanted to on the marketplace, not just upcycled art projects. From there, I asked students to develop a mission statement, slogan, and logo. Together we filled the FH Gizmos homepage with student-written content and products. Students created advertising for FH Gizmos as well as their own individual businesses. With everything in place, we were ready to go to market. In January of 2016, we launched FH Gizmos.

In the six months left of the school year, we made $170, mostly from parents who loved the idea of entrepreneurship in the classroom. In those six months, I saw how entrepreneurship motivated my kids to learn more about computer science, engineering, and digital arts because they needed those skills to develop their products and grow their businesses.

Integrating an EdCorp into Your Curriculum

Before I came to Fair Haven, the classes that now make up my EdCorps program were technology classes. Students worked in computer labs to learn the Microsoft Office suite and touch typing. When I got to Fair Haven, turning these technology classes into a makerspace and eventually EdCorps did not require a total overhaul of the curriculum. The technology standards and topics I was expected to cover paired nicely with an EdCorp. Integrating an EdCorp into your classroom looks different for everyone. That is why I asked some of the talented teachers from across the country who are running EdCorps to share their origin stories and how they integrate and run their programs in more traditional settings and curriculums. As I was reading their stories, I was excited that they also included the different aspects of entrepreneurship in the classroom that have been the most meaningful for them and their students. I have put their stories throughout this book, where they will best show why running an EdCorp is so powerful.

———

Students Catch the Entrepreneurship Bug
Authors: Brooke Tobia & Students
EdCorps: Milkweed for Monarchs
School: Calavera Hills Middle School
Location: Carlsbad, CA
Grade/Subject: Sixth Grade Math

This year, the CHMS sixth grade class has been given an amazing opportunity. Our teachers wanted to show us the relevance of learning sixth-grade concepts while applying them to something meaningful, so we started a business with the help of

Real World Scholars. Our idea was first formed by our Environmental Science class, calling out for a need for help. The class proposed the problem and possible solution to the entire sixth grade through a video about Monarch Butterflies.

Creating and running a business has allowed us to learn many things in different ways. It's been great to be able to incorporate many of our sixth-grade math standards into our business in a way that makes learning fun and interesting. For example, when learning about percents and profit margins, we focused on what percent of profits we would like to use on different things. One idea that we have come up with is using our profits to help fund people on KIVA, an organization that allows us to help others around the world. Our teacher also taught us how to create a P and L sheet (Profit and Loss Sheet). We used this idea to support our learning about adding, subtracting, multiplying, and dividing decimals. There have been so many examples of how we incorporated math into our business that we felt it would be best to list them.

Things we have done in math for our business:

- Percents: Finding out the percentage of the Cost of Goods to the Total Cost. This allowed us to see where most of our money is being spent when making the product.
- Ratios: Ratios are measuring and comparing one thing to another. We worked with ratios in our business when we found the ratios to seeds to soil to clay.
- CoGs(Cost of Goods): How much the materials used to make the product cost. We use this to determine a reasonable price for our products!
- Rates: Rate is the process we used to find unit rates in our business. We learned that we could divide decimals as well. That helped us to a great extent because we needed to know that before ratios!

- Proportions: A proportion is when you write a ratio as a fraction, a different way of seeing a ratio.
- Best packaging options: Finding out what packaging options are the cheapest and best deal. We use this to get the best boxes for the cheapest price so we can use our money on other things.
- Best Priced Materials: Finding the cheapest materials for the best deal. We use this so we can get the cheapest materials for the best quality.
- Unit Rate/Unit Cost: How much something will cost for one item. We use this so we know how much it cost for one item if there is more than one in the pack.
- Total sale: After we find the cost of what it takes to make the product, we have to add a profit. After we add the profit, we get the total sales price.
- Operating Expenses: The operating expenses and losses. The operating expenses are how much money we used for advertising and showing off our business. Operating loss is how much we lose from our profit when doing that. It is very important to have a large enough profit for the operating losses.
- Inventory: How much of the product we have in stock/made! This helps us keep track of sales and keep up with making products.

Izzy and Ariana
Sixth-grade students at CHMS

———

LIKE IZZY AND ARIANA, many of my students were bitten by the entrepreneurship bug. In the Fall of 2017, I was spending my afternoons working with fifth and sixth graders in the Innovation Lab, my mornings were spent working in the elementary school. As FH Gizmos grew in middle school, I was approached by some of my students' younger siblings in the third grade. They heard what we were doing at the middle school, and they wanted to run a business, too.

With third graders in tow, we pitched our principal, Cheryl Cuddihy, on the idea. Students left that meeting with a $75 loan and an Oriental Trading magazine to get their pop-up store off the ground. Students handpicked and ordered inventory they thought their peers would like, they decorate an old rolling cart we found to be our storefront and hung up flyers announcing the FH Gizmos pop-up shop was coming. For the rest of the school year, these dedicated students sacrificed their lunch and recess every Tuesday and Thursday to run the store. Afterward, they counted the money they made, entered it into the ledger, and delivered it to our school secretary to be deposited. They also created a purchase order for the secretary so she could reorder inventory for our store.

The FH Gizmos pop-up shop grew so popular we had to hire more third graders! I asked each third-grade teacher to recommend a student from their class who didn't like math. These new student-employees may have hated math to start, but their attitudes changed fast when they realized they are doing math with the money they've earned. By the end of our time together, they were keeping a spreadsheet that had them not just doing addition and subtraction, but also division, multiplication, and percentages. Using our sheet, students decided what the next steps would be for our business.

Reimagining our EdCorp

The entire FH Gizmos entrepreneurship experience was so rewarding, I wanted to share it with other educators. I wrote an article about FH Gizmos and entrepreneurship in the classroom for EdSurge, a popular edtech blog. Serendipitously, this article was read by the fine folks at Real World Scholars (RWS). The founders of RWS, John and Elyse, reached out to me and shared what they do. RWS provides funding and support for K-12 teachers who want to start student-run businesses, called EdCorps, in their classrooms.

John and Elyse asked if FH Gizmos would be interested in becoming an EdCorp.

Now part of the Real World Scholars family, we started the new school year ready to take FH Gizmos to the next level. Because I had new fifth graders and my now sixth graders are the ones who came up with the idea for FH Gizmos, we started the year by reimagining our business. If it could be anything, what would we want FH Gizmos to be? We decided that we wanted to use design thinking, something I'd been teaching them in the Innovation Lab, in our school and community to find and solve people's problems. If we believed the solution to the problem could help others, we would sell it. This idea of finding problems then creating and selling the solution gave birth to our slogan: Your problem is our project!

The first six months of FH Gizmos focused on interviewing potential customers to understand the problems they face and ensure our solution met their needs. User interviews are one of the most important parts of the product development process for an EdCorp because user interviews help students gain empathy for their potential customers and their needs while also serving as a launching point for brainstorming, prototyping, and testing possible solutions.

We found a lot of problems that needed solving and even managed to solve quite a few of them. When we failed to solve a problem, students were still learning, and I was excited to see them begin to reframe failure as iteration. Our time in class went on like this through winter break.

As Spring came around, so did the fidget spinners craze. They were everywhere. It wasn't long before most teachers banned them from classrooms across the country. I believe in taking what kids are passionate about and using that to engage them in learning. Instead of banning spinner, I embraced them. I created a design challenge for students that asked them to make a fidget spinner that solved a problem. My favorite solution was a fidget spinner that when spun charged your cell phone.

We posted our fidget spinner prototypes to Twitter. A few days later, I found myself in a conversation with a friend and former educator, Kristen Swanson, who worked at Slack. I had originally called her to see if I could use Slack, a cloud-based team collaboration tool, with students to help them learn asynchronous work skills, but the conversation turned toward the fidget spinner prototypes I had posted on Twitter.

I told Kristin the story of how I was incorporating entrepreneurship into my classroom. She loved the idea so much she offered to make Slack FH Gizmos' first big customer!

We Land our First Major Client

In April 2017, we started our Slack Design Challenge.

To help us kick off the empathy phase of our design process, Slack sent over a video outlining their needs and constraints. Slack challenged my students to design something to help employees focus while they were learning in their new education center that could also make a great gift for new employees.

Every class until the end of the year, students prototyped and tested what they thought would be the perfect solution for Slack. Students did sketching, basic CAD design, built prototypes out of cardboard, and found local users to test with. Every team designed what they thought would be the perfect solution, and then we came together and voted on the ten prototypes we would mail to Slack. A week later, Slack let us know they liked our S-shaped fidget spinner the best.

With the school year coming to a close, the students of FH Gizmos came together in a mad dash to find a manufacturer who would be willing to turn our fidget spinner prototype into a finished, professional product. With the help of our state manufacturing cooperative, we found a manufacturer to create the 50 fidget spinners we needed to fill the order for Slack. While they waited for the spinners to be made, students talked pricing, developed packaging, created marketing plans to reach other potential customers, and even made some cold calls to see if our local toy stores would be interested in carrying our fidget spinners. Even the email updates they wrote to Slack were awesome. My students' writing had never been better than when they understood a real person would read their writing, and a well-written email or pitch could be the difference between success and failure. These kids were driven! But then, disaster struck.

We had told Slack the fidget spinners would be shipped by the last day of school, but the production was delayed a week. We missed our deadline. While I was disappointed the kids wouldn't be able to send Slack the finished fidget spinners themselves, I figured I would just box them up, send them, and share the pictures on the class Instagram. But another week went by, then a month, then it was August. No fidget spinners. The manufacturer who agreed to help us kept giving me different reasons they weren't done, until one day in August, he simply said he had to close his shop and couldn't complete the order. We had just gone from fulfilling a manufacturing contract with a huge client to being back where we started in June.

Slack, let it be known, was nothing but wonderful and understanding through this whole ordeal. They, too, understood how much authentic learning projects like this, even in failure, taught students. But I can't lie: we were crushed.

To start the 2018 school year off, I explained to my returning students the situation we were in. Together, we drafted another email to the manufacturing cooperative explaining what happened. In late September, we heard back from VEP Manufacturing. Not only would they remake the fidget spinners on rush, but they would also cover the costs. Four weeks later, we had our gorgeous, engraved red and blue Slack fidget spinners and were finally able to fill our order. For our hard work, Slack paid us a $1000 that we reinvested into our businesses. We were thrilled.

Three Tenets of Entrepreneurship in the Classroom

Three tenets make entrepreneurship in the classroom a great learning tool.

Entrepreneurship is a mirror

The first is that entrepreneurship is a mirror. Entrepreneurship is a mirror because it reflects your effort and attitude. What you put into your business, you will get out of it. And only you can put the time and energy into your business to make it successful. I talk about my class being a mirror to students constantly. It is my way of reminding them that if they want to be successful, it is up to them. If their business is not successful, then they need only look in the mirror for someone to blame.

The beauty in entrepreneurship being a mirror is that it helps students build confidence. Especially at the middle school level, confidence seems to be in short supply. Often, students would rather do nothing than do something wrong. They regurgitate the knowledge we feed them. They write or say what they think we want to hear. Through entrepreneurship, I have seen students become more confident.

Entrepreneurship is a silo buster

Beyond being a mirror, entrepreneurship makes learning a silo-busting experience. Nothing else forces a student to combine and use their prior knowledge like entrepreneurship. To be successful, students have to draw on everything they've learned in their educational career, break this knowledge out of the silos we teach them in, and apply them to the problems they face and the goals they set while running their business. Siloed subjects such as math, literacy, art, public speaking, history, and science need to be used in an EdCorp classroom for students' businesses to be successful.

Entrepreneurship makes learning real and relevant

Finally, we know that students learn more when learning is authentic.

We hear a lot about authentic learning, but it is a term that needs to be unpacked to understand how entrepreneurship fits into the equation. What makes learning authentic? Learning is authentic when it is real and relevant.

My students run real businesses that solve real problems while trying to turn a real profit. Nothing about my class is fake or manufactured. The problems are real. The success is real. The failure is real. And real does not mean easy. Little of what happens in the EdCorp classroom is easy. The real problems we find or face are difficult, sticky, wicked problems.

The learning is also relevant. When we make something relevant for our kids, significant learning takes place because people will self-educate around a topic if it is presented to them in a context that they enjoy. Many reluctant writers in my class have no problem writing pitches or product descriptions when it is for their business. My students who hate math love to calculate their profit margins and, most of all, count the money they've made.

Real and relevant entrepreneurship allows students to break down learning silos and see how their effort and passion can make a real difference. There is no better vehicle for our kids to stretch themselves and develop the skills it takes to be successful — not just in school or business, but in life too —than entrepreneurship. All you have to do is guide them.

Chapter 2

BECOMING THE CHIEF OPPORTUNITY ORCHESTRATOR

Teacher: Jennifer Stillittano
EdCorps: Dire Lights
School: Central Coast New Tech High School
Location: Nipomo, CA
Grade/Subject: Entrepreneurship

The entrepreneurial journey of the student-run EdCorp, Dire-Lights, started in a coffee shop in San Diego. Like many great innovations, this one was fueled by early morning caffeine and a strong sense of excitement as I was on my way to the Deeper Learning Conference in 2017. To fully understand the Dire-Lights story, we must go back in time to 2011. My direct experience with entrepreneurship started the moment I said yes to joining the innovative and dynamic team of seven people who would later become the founding staff members of Central Coast New Tech High School in Nipomo, California.

Soon after the work of starting a new school began, I became aware of the mindsets and skills that develop in a person who is part of starting something from nothing. While I was not assuming the financial risk that entrepreneurs usually do, by being part of the team to start our school, there were numerous other risks I had to take to help design and build a school that aligned with my vision of the way school should be. Some of the characteristics gained by overcoming the obstacles that we faced to achieve our vision included: initiative/self-reliance, flexibility/adaptability, communication, collaboration, critical thinking, problem-solving, recognizing opportunities, goal setting/future-oriented thinking, comfort with risk, creativity, and innovation. As we were building, we were constantly reflecting, and I couldn't help but realize that the knowledge, skills, and attributes required to start the school (business) were almost exactly the same understandings we desired to instill in our future students (clients). Creating a school that would "ignite creativity, empower through authenticity, and provide learning experiences for the 21st century" meant providing our students with an engaging, challenging, and inspiring environ-ment through which they become empowered and contributing members of our society. It clicked, doing real work that we are deeply passionate about and engaged in is how we learn best. So, then the challenge became how do I translate this experi-ence and the idea of doing real, authentic work to my classroom.

Seven years later, in that coffee shop is where the answers came together, and my old New Tech Network coach, friend, and teacherpreneur herself, Jenny Pieratt of CraftEd Curriculum, introduced me to Elyse Burden co-founder of Real World Scholars. As a project-based learning facilitator and trainer, I knew that getting the grant and support from Real World Scholars was my ticket to bringing a truly authentic project to my students. Getting my students to actually do real work takes capital and networking. Ironically, the connections between starting and running a business and my classroom are countless.

The significance of authenticity in any high-quality company is also a core principle of designing an engaging, project-based learning experience for students. Authenticity is arguably the most significant element of project design. As one of the "A's" from the New Tech Network 6A's of project design, authenticity, was my main focus for my entrepreneurial mindsets course. By designing curriculum the "new tech way," I also was able to ensure my projects intentionally incorporated the other "A's": academic rigor, applied learning, active exploration, adult connections, and assessment practices that are student-centered and require the meaningful use of technology. As soon as Real World Scholars and I started emailing, it was a remarkably easy process to get the logistical elements of our EdCorp, Dire-Lights, up and running. After an encouraging phone interview with Audrey Reimer and a convincing conversation I had to have with my school district's assistant superintendent, I received funding, and the rest was now in my hands. Inspired by the New Tech Network and the ideas of Ron Berger, I now had the chance to make my classroom a place where students were deeply learning by doing real, authentic work. I spent the summer before launching our EdCorp thinking and dreaming a lot! Like all great entrepreneurs and teachers, I knew I had to dream big, yet also focus on my exit strategy, I had to begin with the end in mind.

I recognized the importance of the collaborative process of ideation as a component of being a successful entrepreneur, but the class business could not be the place to let that happen. Logistically, I knew that if I used class time to let this first year's students decide what to create a business around, I would be wasting a lot of time talking and dreaming instead of doing. Over the past decade, project-based learning has become a way of thinking for me, and so I knew I could design the aspect of ideation, brainstorming, and creativity in other areas of the year. I also knew the business had to be something that I was interested in; after all, these students would be with me and the business for a year, but then they would leave and move on, leaving next year's students and me to continue to run and grow the enterprise. I also realized that whatever we created needed to be relatively easy for anyone to make and safely producible within the walls of my classroom. The idea of hand-poured soy wax candles came to me after days and days of talking to everyone I knew about this amazing opportunity and reflecting on my own ability to craft and make in my own kitchen. I had dabbled in candle making for the past several years as a way to mix up the gift-giving I did over the holiday season. Candles! It was perfect! They are relatively cheap and easy to produce; if I could do it, I knew my students could, too. I decided that the student voice and choice and ownership over the business would be to take my simple idea and make it grow so it could actually happen. They would find the ownership and buy-in by personalizing the entire process and making it their own.

DireLights was born, and I started the school year building trust and culture with my crew of kiddos. I had to get to know them well and help us all build trusting relationships with each other before allowing them to start and manage this business. By launching the course with an entry event describing the grant I received from RWS and the idea I had for a candle company, students were called to action to fulfill the challenge of starting and running CCNTH's first-ever student-run enterprise. They were excited and ready to start, and I was confident that the thought and work I put into designing my course over the summer was going to pay off.

The best way to explain how I applied the New Tech Network model of PBL to my EdCorp is by describing how I organized the year of learning for my Entrepreneurial Mindsets students. I divided the course into three projects. The first project titled, *Entrepreneurial Mindsets Gallery,* asked students to create a final product of their choice and deliver a professional presentation in front of a panel of teachers, parents, and local business experts that answered the driving question: "What makes someone an entrepreneur?" The major goals of my first project were to build trusting relationships with this group of students and help them self-identify their strengths, skills, interests, and challenges all in order to place students in the correct position in the business, DireLights. I introduced students to this first project through an entry event which consisted of a mini-debate around the question of who the most impactful entrepreneur of all time is, living or dead, and then I had them read the entry doc:

Dear Students,

This first project is your chance to make a first impression and investigate what it takes to become a successful entrepreneur. During this project, I will be observing you to determine who will be best suited for certain positions in the company, DireLights.

I will need you to think about the following questions:

- *What makes someone an entrepreneur?*
- *What are the mindsets and traits of an entrepreneur, and do I have them?*
- *How do history and the economy affect entrepreneurship?*
- *What does it mean to think globally and act locally?*
- *How do we determine the best type of business for our ideas?*
- *How do effective entrepreneurs communicate?*
- *How do ethics and social responsibility affect entrepreneurship?*

I am truly honored and excited to be part of this learning journey with each and every one of you. We will discover what our strengths are and how we can leverage them to get what we want. We will also develop a sense of self- awareness needed to continue growing and developing as our best selves. By June, we will all come closer to understanding what we each need to do in order to live a life of balanced connection and to leave a legacy and an impact on the world that we are proud of.

With Excitement,
Ms. Stillittano

This project required students to complete various benchmarks centered around developing agency skills, like reflecting on their ability to practice a growth mindset and taking ownership of their own learning. Some benchmarks to highlight that worked especially well for transferring the burden of learning from me to my students included: a *Hopes, Notes & Meta-Moments Journal, a Project One Workshop Slidedeck, and a Resume, Cover Letter & Professional Website.* The purpose of the *Hopes, Notes & Meta-Moments Journal* is their place to record wonderings, learnings, and wild ideas as they move through the course. Here I asked them to write, sketch, draw, and brainstorm to help facilitate reflection and help them make the most of their experience. As John Dewey says, experiences are only educative if they lead to further learning and further action. So, having students take notes in order to externalize and make their thinking visible and accountable is a critical skill that successful entrepreneurs exhibit.

Another benchmark to highlight is the *Project Workshop Slidedeck,* which I then use in every other consecutive project of the year. This benchmark asks students to take any of their personal questions or need to knows and then research options and provide an evidence-based answer to each of them. They use a collaborative class slide deck to digitally house and organize their learning and next steps as well as present their findings to the entire class. I also designed a teacher-led workshop on SWOTs & BHAGs (strengths, weaknesses, opportunities, threats, & Big Hairy Audacious Goals) so that I could help students dream big and practice future-oriented thinking as one aspect of the entrepreneurial mindset. The last significant benchmark in the first project also helps foster a sense of goal setting, communication, and adaptability by challenging students to get ready for a job interview with me in the company, DireLights, by updating their resume, professional website, and writing a cover letter customized for the position they desire. Sometimes focusing on authenticity in PBL can force teachers to sacrifice academic rigor and assessment practices, but to combat this, I ask students to complete weekly readings and write reflective blog posts which they publish on their professional websites and discuss every Monday in a Socratic Seminar format. This, too, would continue into the other projects of the course.

After formal presentations to the question *what makes someone an entrepreneur*, and after we have collectively determined who will be taking on what role in the company, our second project begins. *DireLights: Let Some Light In* is the core project that guides students in managing and growing the EdCorp. The driving question students explore for this project is, "What makes a business work?" Their main task in this project is to do the real work of the position they were hired for. During this project, students are responsible for running and growing the DireLights artisan candle company. They were also able to make a personal connection to the project as they self-identified tasks that aligned with their own interests to complete. For example, Matthew Richardson, a student in my course last year, had an interest in graphic design – he was encouraged and hired to explore the role of the graphic designer in the business and also apply his skills to further the project; he ended up creating the DireLights logo and candle label. Each student had a job in the company that utilized their strengths and skills; from Chief Operations Officer (COO) to Social Media Manager, I structured the EdCorp like a real corporation. They were also asked to revise and present their sections of the Direlights Business Plan & Business Model Canvas in front of local entrepreneurs as well as practice their position in the company at various CCNTH event nights.

In addition to their work on the business plan and canvas, they were asked to contribute and update the DireLights Company Playbook to reflect what they've learned about the practices and processes of running our business through the lens of their individual position in the company. The Playbook will be used by the new students every year and updated to reflect the most recent growth and trends of our company.

The benchmarks that I designed to intentionally ask students to tap into the entrepreneurial mindsets of self-reliance and initiative included: *Interview Takeaways* and *Project Management Goals & Timeline*. Here I purposefully wanted to sprinkle some adult connections in with the authenticity of running a real business. Students were exposed to guest experts through speakers that I invited in to discuss their views on the entrepreneurial mindset, but they also had to choose someone to interview who would specifically help them do their job better in the company. Some highlights from this project included fostering a strong sense of agency and collaboration by assigning students scaffolds like creating a physical SCRUM board in the classroom and discovering how to take big goals and divide them up into manageable tasks. Responsibility and commitment, along with being proactive in business rather than reactive, are core traits I hope to instill in my kiddos. The *DireLights: Let Some Light In* project is really where the magic happened. Students felt empowered and passionate about their role in making the business run smoothly and turn a profit. Observing my students in this project, I was hard-pressed to see the difference between a local candle startup or a high school classroom. Teenagers doing authentic work to learn and grow their skills within a safe space...pure magic.

Two other notable elements of the second project, *DireLights: Let Some Light In,* are peer feedback strategies to help facilitate effective collaboration and useful critiques of work. Getting people to collaborate effectively can be very tricky, and using strategies and protocols can help take the potential of hurt feelings and defensiveness out of the equation. Having students regularly score and give feedback to each other on their collaboration skills helps to curb common dysfunctions of a team from arising. They can hold themselves and their teammates accountable safely and constructively by using a collaboration rubric and using it to score each other at various points in the project. The second strategy is the critical friends protocol that we use to ensure respectful, meaningful critiques of work. In order to facilitate peer-to-peer feedback on student work, not behavior, that is actually meaningful and moves beyond the typical "good job" or "nice work," students act as "critical friends" and offer "likes, wonders, and next steps" that push thinking and result in useful revisions of work.

In addition to these required elements, I offered some additional learning extensions or deep dives to differentiate my project further. The deep dives are to keep a Project Management Log of hours worked and submit it with each benchmark deadline to receive payment. I use fake money if they take advantage of this learning extension, and then they can redeem a prize of their choice using company funds. The other deep dive wants students to read and/or watch any approved book or movie that relates to our course content and write an additional blog post about it. Project-Based Learning makes it easy to differentiate and personalize instruction by incorporating a fair amount of student voice and choice and reflection into the curriculum.

I designed the last project of the year with the specific goals of getting my students to bring their creativity, critical thinking, and problem-solving all together. Students are asked to answer the driving question, "how do we design a business we are passionate about?" in the project titled *Plan It, Pitch It!* In this last project of the year, students are challenged to exhibit the entrepreneurial mindset of ideation to develop a business model canvas and business pitch presentation for an idea of their own that they are passionate about. My BHAG (Big Hairy Audacious Goal) for this project is that students actually complete the beginning steps of starting their own profitable business that they can continue building into their college years and beyond. How cool would it be if they start a business with me, and it actually starts making them money to get through college?! The key benchmarks I designed in this last project to highlight were the *Rough Draft and Peer Review of the BMC (business model canvas) & Pitch Presentation.* First, students took time to reflect on their learning from the first and second project and identify key takeaways and understandings that they could now apply to their own idea for a business. For students to complete this project successfully, they needed to use strategies they learned earlier in the year, for example, how to identify what they already know and then what they need to know to create project goals and timeline of tasks that needed to be completed.

They also needed to apply the principles of opportunity recognition, ethics, and communication to the work of developing their own business. This last project allowed me to finish off the year, emphasizing creativity, critical thinking, and problem-solving.

Acknowledging that the world's best teachers are the ones that are continuing to learn and grow themselves, I challenge you to identify your own need to knows about project-based learning and the entrepreneurial mindset and spend some time reflecting on how to bring the idea of having students do work that really matters into your own classroom.

So, after only one year since the inception of DireLights, we have turned a profit, doubled in company size, and brought a structure to Central Coast New Tech High that is an authentic and sustainable way for students to learn about entrepreneurship by actually doing it. Our next steps include eventually working with our new Makerspace on campus as well as connecting with students in the digital media arts pathway for marketing and branding growth. We also will continue to foster our relationship between Cal Poly's Center for Innovation and Entrepreneurship and Cuesta College. What about you? How can you apply the core principles of Project-Based Learning to your classroom to help foster the entrepreneurial mindset in yourself and your students?

———

Jennifer's journey in starting her EdCorp is a lot like my own. It will probably be a lot like yours, too: exciting, overwhelming, and full of uncertainty. At least that's how I felt when the year after starting our first EdCorp, I was given the opportunity to expand the program.

On the back of the success of FH Gizmos, I was asked to expand the FH Gizmos experience into a schoolwide program for all of our fourth through eighth-grade students. In September 2018, I launched the Fair Haven Innovates program. The FH Innovates program is Fair Haven school district's 21st-century life, innovation, and technology program. We use social entrepreneurship, a business model that puts 'doing good' for others as its core belief, to help students learn the skills and have the experiences they'll need to be successful. In FH Innovates, students find problems and sell the solutions as they run real businesses that turn a real profit.

I pushed our makerspace, the Innovation Lab, down to fourth and fifth grade. The Innovation Lab is our farm league where fourth and fifth-grade students are introduced to design thinking, engineering, computer science, and the digital arts through project-based learning. The goal of the Innovation Lab is to help students reframe failure as iteration, learn to work as a team, and gain empathy by teaching them how to walk in someone else's shoes.

Sixth graders still run FH Gizmos. In FH Gizmos, students form problem-solving teams that go out into their school and community to help others. If the solutions to these problems are successful, we sell them. In FH Gizmos, your problem is still our project.

In FH Grows, my seventh-grade EdCorp, we learn to be stewards of the environment while leveraging technology to help our garden and business grow. We sell our herbs and produce online and in our student-run farmer's market to restaurants and community members. When we're not working in the gardens, FH Grows is trying to work on environmental issues like food deserts, sustainable farming, renewable energy, and how to clean up our polluted land and water.

FH Leads is our eighth-grade incubator EdCorp where students start businesses they can take with them when they graduate. Many students choose to start businesses that improve their community.

Fair Haven Innovates		
The Innovation Lab	Fourth and Fifth Grade	A blended-learning makerspace with a focus on skill development
FH Gizmos	Sixth Grade	Students act as problem finders as they try to develop products that solve people's problems
FH Grows	Seventh Grade	Agriculture meets technology as students start businesses around environmental issues
FH Leads	Eighth Grade	A business incubator where students can start their own business they take with them when they graduate

Running an EdCorp is a lot like running a project-based learning (PBL) classroom. By the time I got to Fair Haven, I had four years of PBL experience under my belt, which helped me manage the EdCorp experience. But while a lot of the best practices for PBL work in the EdCorp classroom, there are some additional best practices you'll need to be successful. You need to become the COO of the classroom—the Chief Opportunity Orchestrator.

Becoming the COO of my EdCorps required me to change how I saw my role in the classroom and what I believed learning looked like. For the first five years of my teaching career, I refused to give up ownership of my classroom. I believed I always had to be in charge. I had to have every minute students spent in the classroom planned out. I micromanaged students, and I was often the only voice heard in the classroom. My class was often a PowerPoint lecture followed by student-regurgitation in an essay or test format. Silence and compliance – these are what I believed a classroom was supposed to look like. The reality was that my students were miserable, and you know what, so was I. Teaching had become a chore.

The summer before my sixth year teaching, I did some heavy reflection, personal learning, and networking with educators I admired. What I came away with at the end of the summer was this: my kids wanted to do something cool, I just had to get out of their way.

I wasn't ready to give up control all at once, but I made a promise to myself that I would give up some of my classroom time so students could explore their passions. To do that, I started the Be About It project. The Be About It project was my way of allowing students to take ownership of their learning and explore things that they were passionate about. I gave students one day a week, all year, to make something. Students could work with whom they wanted, where they wanted, and on what they wanted. The only thing I asked was that at the end of the year, they would get up on stage and tell us what they did, why they did it, and what they learned.

Initially, students approached the project with trepidation and choice paralysis. Instead of doing something wrong, some of my kids preferred to do nothing. They were so well trained in *doing school* —to do exactly what they were told and to get the grade that they wanted— they were scared of the project. They thought that it had to be a trick. But the *Be About It* project gave me time to meet with each kid. As I sat with my kids, something became clear: most of my kids weren't passionate about anything.

Passion takes time and experience to develop. My students struggled to find their passion likely because they have spent most of their educational careers doing what they were told. Never had my kids been given the opportunity, without the chokehold of grades or threat of failure, to explore their interests in hopes of finding their passion. How can we expect them to develop passion if we don't let them explore? They had interests. They had causes they cared about it. They had slices of life that made them happy, mad, and inspired them, but, ultimately, when asked about their passions, they shrugged. When I reframed the project as a chance to find out what they were passionate about, students looked at the project as an opportunity to find the things that matter to them. Students were more willing to try when I asked them what they cared about, what interested them, or what made them mad. At the end of the year, this shift in framing was clear. Onstage, many students shared that they *didn't* find what they were passionate about, but they *did* find what they were not passionate about. One student thought she wanted to go to vocational school to be a chef. Her project was to create a cookbook with her favorite foods, which she would make for her friends and family. During her presentation, she got up on stage and proudly announced that she didn't want to be a chef anymore. In fact, she said, she hates cooking. In a world where most students go to college not knowing what they want to do and 33 percent of students end up changing their major, I was just as happy that my students found what they didn't want to be as much as when students find the opposite. I was proud that my students were changing their majors or post-high school trajectory before they even graduated.

In a classroom where the teacher shares control, the teacher must able be to give feedback and help steer students constantly. Outlining manageable chunks of the Be About It projects helped them stay focused. I rarely revealed more than two weeks of expectations to students. They told me that seeing the whole year laid out made them feel overwhelmed. Even a monthly calendar of checkpoints was too much. Two weeks seemed to be the sweet spot. Over the six years I've spent giving up control of my classroom, my ability to hold students accountable has continued to get better and better. In the assessment section later in the book, I will dive into the best practices that I've developed through this project and over the years to help you hold students accountable.

During the project, I would joke with students about how the Be About It project was actually *my* Be About It project. I would talk to students about what I was doing well and what I was doing poorly since it was my first time running the Be About It project. Soon I realized students were tuned in to how I was handling change, overcoming adversity, and navigating uncertainty as I was modeling the Be About It project. I often apologized to my kids, sharing my screw-ups, or ways I wanted to do things better. Each week, I would change the way I assessed students to help them achieve their goals. One week I said no cell phones; the next week, I allowed cell phones because it made the project better. I opened up social media, I allowed students to create personal email accounts. My students got more comfortable with being uncomfortable, and I realized that it was because of how I was modeling that for them.

Eventually, most students became independent, self-starters. They didn't burn down the classroom or sit around and do nothing. They worked hard to make their projects a reality. My role as the Chief Opportunity Orchestrator grew out of the *Be About It* project. Over the last three years, I have learned how to manage a project-based classroom where students are all working on different projects. I developed and refined a process that kept me up-to-date on what students were doing in class, kept them on task, and had them producing artifacts that showed their learning (you can find these in the resource section). The project changed me as an educator, shifting what I thought my role was and what I believed about learning altogether.

Having a belief is an act of faith. There are four beliefs I have about the classroom that give me faith in my kids and their ability to be more than the sum of their parts. I truly believe to run an EdCorp, you have to adopt these beliefs and become the one looking for opportunities for learning. If you do, you will retire your ideas of what it means to be a teacher, shoot right past Guide on the Side, and become the Chief Opportunity Orchestrator.

Belief One: Let Your Kids Lead the Way

When students are pursuing an opportunity, the job of the COO is to guide them toward success by giving them the feedback, resources, time, and tools they need to be successful in their goals. Easy enough, right? Well, here's the hard part: you can't hold their hand.

As the COO, it is important to keep your kids moving forward, guiding them toward success, through all the adversity that comes with being an entrepreneur. Understand, though, our job is to create the conditions where success is possible, not to make sure students are successful. Success is up to them because entrepreneurship is a mirror. I do everything I can to guide my kids toward success, but they must ultimately be the ones that define it and go for it. I curate resources and experts. I give advice, suggestions, and differing points of view. I suggest the next steps and give feedback. But I do not give in to learned helplessness, and I will not *do* things for students. You will experience a lot of this learned helplessness when you start because most students haven't worked autonomously before. By helping students understand that discomfort is often a feeling they'll have when learning something new, you will be able to harness that anxiety and channel into their success.

When we let students become the captains of their own ship, we teach them that their success is their responsibility, and we empower them to create their own opportunities. A lot of the opportunities we find don't always work out. We email people and never hear back. Timelines, deadlines, or the cost of a project sometimes are not feasible. And there are times that we just fail outright. For example, we worked with our local hospital this year and weren't able to solve any of their challenges. Not one. We still learned a lot, but we failed at our original goal. That's because the core of the entrepreneurial process is this: helping students understand that failing is fine as long as they've learned something is important. Failure is best viewed as a temporary state, a stepping stone to ultimate success. This flies in the face of how we often hear students make sense of failure: the teacher doesn't like me. I didn't understand. I don't care.

An added bonus to letting your kids lead the way is how often they will surprise you. Your kids want to do something awesome; you just have to get out of their way. For me, this was letting kids start the *Parts to Arts* initiative. It was supporting my kids when they suggested selling their art, even though I didn't know how it was going to end. But it let them take ownership of their learning. Sometimes, students ignore my feedback and fail miserably. Other times, they go their own way, and it works out better. Either way, letting kids lead the way means supporting them even if you don't understand or agree with what they're doing. The reality is that kids learn by doing. They learn when they make mistakes. Your goal as the COO should be to identify opportunities for students to get as much real-world experience (and learning experience) as possible before they graduate. This is only possible if we let them lead the way.

Belief Two: Making is the Best Learning

The COO of an EdCorp must believe that those who are doing the making are doing the learning. Making time for making is the most basic way to transfer ownership of learning from teacher to student and build your students' creative confidence. As you combine your curriculum with the key activities of running an EdCorp, a concept I will address later, you must find ways for your students to make during class.

It may sound like a tall order, but making doesn't have to come all at once. At first, being the COO and letting my kids make was just a part-time thing. When I was teaching high school English, I first introduced making by replacing a few assessments with student-made creations like screencasts, infographics, and board games that took the place of traditional testing. Next, I stopped assigning essays and had my students blog instead. Students blogged about topics, reflections, and reactions to what they were learning in class. In these instances, the move toward making was gradual. The success of these eventually led me to start asking students: how would you like to show me what you learned?

"How would you like to show me what you learned?" was an invitation for students to make. It represented the transfer of full ownership of their learning over to them. It was the ultimate push toward creative confidence. They came up with their own projects, solved problems they cared about, and shared their passions with the world. I got a ton of mileage out of that question. This exercise and the practice of making helped me identify new opportunities for them, further transitioning me into my emerging COO role. Start replacing traditional assessments by allowing students to make something, anything. Next, start asking your kids how they'd like to share what they've learned. From there, next thing you know, your class may look a lot like a makerspace where content knowledge collides with the opportunity for students to create.

Belief Three: You Don't Have to Be the Expert

Letting students lead means that they are going to lead me down paths outside of my expertise and into areas I know nothing about. That's OK. In fact, it's great. When I get to learn something new, it allows me to model facing discomfort and lifelong learning for my kids. For example, when my students suggested starting our agriculture EdCorp, FH Grows, I had no gardening experience. I contacted our state Department of Agriculture, who put me in touch with Rutgers University, who put me in touch with the Rutgers Master Gardeners program. Since FH Grows started, the Master Gardeners have been working with my kids and me. Before we knew it, a gap in our expertise became an opportunity to connect with real experts and learn in a different way and from other people. Creating new opportunities for your students means being comfortable learning alongside students, together. It means saying, "I don't know, but let's find out together." It means saying, "I've taken you as far as I can; we'll need to find someone else to take us further together." You become the COO when you make connections – and help students make connections – with people and resources that can help them achieve their goals.

While you don't have to be the expert on everything, you do need to know how to find the experts. You need to open your classroom to those who can share their experiences and expertise with your students. One way to find experts is by using a technique I call *carpet emailing*. Carpet emailing involves finding as many people's emails at the organization you want to contact and emailing them all. In the email, I explain who I am, what we do, and what help we are looking for. The key sentence is this: "if you're not the right person to ask, could you put me in contact with the person who is?" It never fails—eventually, someone always gets back to me. And more times than not, they couldn't be happier to help or refer me to someone who can.

Carpet emailing works great; reaching out to experts on social media is even better. Many experts and organizations are extra helpful on social media because it's happening in a public square; they know everyone can see the interaction, and they want to reap the social capital of helping students: everyone is happy to help because it's for the kids!

How you ask experts for help is important, too. You need to be clear in what you are asking for. Since you will most likely be asking for someone's time, you must respect their time by laying out what you want and how long it will take. Be clear about what you've already done. People are much more likely to help if you've already put in some sweat equity. For instance, when we want help with packaging, students send pictures of prototypes they've made. Because students have already done some of the legwork, people are more likely to help. When you ask for help, have something started: a rough draft, a prototype, or anything else you can show someone to help convey your vision and show how serious you are.

Finally, opportunities are reciprocal. The COO does everything in its power to make the relationship beneficial to both parties. You and your students should find ways to give back and promote the causes of the people and groups who step up to support your students. Let them know how you'll give back during the ask. This can serve as a powerful reminder to your students that they also have something to offer, right here and now.

One last thing to keep in mind: assisting students in being resourceful and finding their own experts is important. Even though you will need to vet anyone who your students ultimately contact, you can put them in the driver's seat as they use email and social media to craft their own asks. Experiences like this give students real-world opportunities to find their voice and their confidence, not to mention honing things like professional communication skills.

Chapter 3

LAUNCHING YOUR EDCORP

One of the first things the Chief Opportunity Orchestrator needs to decide is the structure of their EdCorp, the type of model the COO will use to run their business. The main variables to consider when picking a model is the number of students you see and the frequency with which you see them. For example, as a sophomore English teacher, I saw kids every other day for 90 minutes. Because I saw kids so frequently and for an extended period, I let them start and run their own businesses. When I started out at Fair Haven, I saw every kid in the school – more than 600 students – once every six days. Seeing so many kids for such a short time, it was best if we all ran an EdCorp together. Having taught with so many different schedules and class sizes, I've found three structures work best:

EdCorps Structures	
Amazon-style	Students create products. Teacher handles marketing, sales, and finance aspects of the business with some help from students.
Decentralized-style	Students create products. Students handle marketing, sales, and finance aspects of the business. Teacher takes on a support role with equal power to students.
Incubator-style	Students create and run their own businesses under one EdCorp umbrella. Students handle every aspect of their own business. Teacher takes on a support role, but has no power over students' business. Teacher should help students when needed.

FH Gizmos: The Amazon-style EdCorps

In FH Gizmos, students set out to find and solve problems and then sell the solutions. All students are part of a product team, and when they have a product ready to sell, it goes on the online FH Gizmos marketplace. When a customer visits the website, they see all of the solutions FH Gizmos product teams have created. Like Amazon, FH Gizmos is a marketplace.

I am in charge of FH Gizmos. Students create the products while I handle most of the day-to-day operations of the EdCorps, such as marketing. When it is time to sell a product, it is marketed as part of the FH Gizmos family of products. The FH Gizmos model is focused primarily on the design of new products and the experience of collaborating in teams.

If the entrepreneurial process is new to you as an educator, this EdCorp structure can be a great way to get started as it eases the class into a more student-driven environment while allowing the teacher to retain most of the control.

FH Grows: The Whole-Grade (Decentralized-style) EdCorps

In FH Grows, students sell herbs and produce to restaurants and community members in our town. Every student is responsible for maintaining our gardens. When we have downtime in the garden, my seventh graders are responsible for growing our business. Teams take on a "department" role in areas they are interested in. I choose to let students stay in these departments as long as they like because growing student passion and developing expertise is important for middle schoolers. You can, however, rotate students through departments if you want them to try out each department.

The Design department is responsible for creating products for FH Grows to sell. The design department surveys the community to get a feel for what they might want to buy. Students have come up with products such as upcycled planters and garden ornaments, holiday flowers, spring vegetable starters, catnip bags, worm farms, and organic seed packets. The Design team is responsible for using our design process to create new and exciting products to sell alongside the produce we harvest from our garden.

People can't support your business if they don't know it exists. Our Marketing department is responsible for developing creative, engaging ways to tell the community the FH Grows story, which lets them know that we're open for business. It is a two-step process. First, students find the customers that make up our target market using market research, customer segmentation, and community outreach. Once we know who and where our customers are, students advertise our story with a call to action to encourage customers to buy our products.

Once people know our EdCorp exists, the Sales department is responsible for closing deals and generating revenue by helping customers see the value in our products. Whether potential customers visit our website, contact us via email or social media, or even send in a handwritten letter or note with their child: it is the job of the sales team to reach out and make contact with customers. They then move customers through our sales cycle. After a purchase, the sales team is responsible for gathering customer feedback, encouraging future purchases, and generating new leads to explore.

The Design, Marketing, and Sales departments can't be successful without the Finance department. The finance department is responsible for tracking sales and making sure our financials are in order. They manage our ledger, inventory, and work with stakeholders in our district to make sure we have the money we need when we need it. Often, the finance team is tasked with using their creativity to minimize expenses and maximize revenue in FH Grows, which takes critical thinking and creative problem-solving. For example, one of our best-selling products in FH Grows is our worm farms. Students start the worm farm for customers and then give it to customers along with a guide on how to maintain the worm farm and harvest the worm castings for fertilizer. We sell the worm farm for $150. In the beginning, we were only making 33% profit off the worm farms. Not satisfied with the low margin, the finance team found a new worm supplier, explained to them that we are a student-run business, and were able to secure a discount, which brought our profit margin over 50%.

An EdCorp that includes a large group of students or an entire grade and is structured like FH Grows sees the COO move to a support role. The level of control you want to have in this environment is totally up to you, but you can't have total control (nor should you want it). In FH Grows, student teams work together to come up with ideas to grow our business. Then, they pitch them to the rest of the students and me. We hold all-hands meetings where we look at our Business Model Canvas as a simplified, one-page version of our business plan and decide on the next steps. My vote, so long as students aren't proposing something completely egregious, counts just as much as their vote. While I give my thoughts about a proposal, I'm often outvoted. I'm ok with that since half of the time, the ideas I'm outvoted on end up doing well—which is awesome. Students feel empowered and make sure to let me know that their idea worked despite my protests. The other half of the time, the idea fails miserably, and that's fine, too. Failure is a fantastic teacher, and I try to capitalize on these teachable moments as we break down why an idea failed and if there is anything worth saving about the idea.

FH Leads: The Incubator-style EdCorp

In FH Gizmos, my sixth graders answer to me (and their customers, of course). They follow the vision I've laid out for FH Gizmos and focus on creating products rather than running the business. In FH Grows, my seventh graders take on more responsibility as they make grade-wide pitches they think will help our business grow. In this whole-class, whole-grade EdCorp, students take on more ownership of the business since we run it together. In the FH Leads, our incubator-style EdCorp, students take full ownership of their learning because we do not run a business together; they start and run their *own* business.

A business incubator is an organization designed to accelerate the growth of other businesses. In FH Leads, my goal as the COO is to help students start successful businesses that they can take with them when they graduate from middle school.

Students start by deciding on their teammates or co-founders. Next, students find a problem and develop a product or service to solve that problem. When students have a prototype of their product, they do user testing. A user is someone who will benefit from a student's solution. If you develop a better dog leash, you wouldn't test it with someone who doesn't own a dog. User testing consists of putting their prototypes in the hands of users to get feedback. They watch users with their prototype and take notes on how the user reacts to the prototype. They ask users what they like about their prototype, what they would change, and how their prototype compares to the product they are currently using. After a lot of user testing, it is time for students to bring their products or services to market. Student teams create a Business Model Canvas to outline the next steps for their business. When they have a sound business model, they can apply for a business grant to help get their business off the ground. If I approve the grant, I will give them between $50-100, real money, to get their startup going. Students are then responsible for the continued design, marketing, sales, and financing of their business. If I have total control in FH Gizmos, I give up total control in FH

Leads. Students are solely responsible for their business and its success.

To this end, as the COO of FH Leads, I must provide advice and feedback, but also opportunities to hear others' advice and feedback as well. I open up FH Leads to business owners in my community and experts I find worldwide. I have a pool of talented business professionals locally and abroad that can mentor students. Between my support, these mentors, and the experience they've gained in FH Gizmos and FH Grows, most of my students' startups can turn a profit before they graduate.

In my experience, starting a business isn't in every student's wheelhouse. Even though I make it well known that FH Innovates classes are about disrupting the status quo, I still have students who aren't comfortable with being their own boss. Some kids are afraid of failure, others are afraid of success, and some can't find the creative confidence to build a business around solving a problem they care about. That is why if some students in FH Leads don't want to start their own business, they can help a local, small business owner grow their business. If students choose, they can team up with a small business owner – almost like an intern – and help solve the challenges the business owner faces. If students don't want to work for themselves, they have the option to work for someone else. Either way, students are put in a leadership position where they finish out the FH Innovates program in the FH Leads EdCorp, where they are pushed to find the agency needed to be responsible for their own success.

Picking the model that is right for you comes down to how comfortable you are giving up control, class size, how often you see your kids, and the experience level of students. The Amazon-style EdCorp sees a teacher remain in control of the EdCorp. The decentralized style EdCorp puts the teacher on equal footing with students as they make decisions together. Finally, the EdCorp as a business incubator sees the teacher move to a support role while students take complete ownership of their businesses and how it is run. Choose the one that is right based on your comfort level with teaching in an EdCorps. As you get better at being the COO, you can always change the model that best fits your program.

Chapter 4

SILO BUSTING WITH KEY ACTIVITIES

A s you just read, you can start an EdCorp in your classroom in a variety of ways. Once you've established your EdCorp, it is time to focus on the day-to-day activities of your business. I've found that there are certain key activities that a student-run business will need to do (and redo) to be successful. What makes these key activities important, besides their ability to grow your business, is their ability to help you bust down the silos we teach our content in so you can get cross-curricular in your classroom. I break these key activities down for students into three stages: what to do when creating a product, what to do when you have a product to sell, and what to do when you've sold a product.

Key Activities for Creating a Product

A design process is a creative problem-solving process that can be applied to any activity in your EdCorps. We use our design process to create everything from our product to our packaging, marketing campaigns, customer surveys, and everything in-between. Every problem we face or when we're not sure about our next steps, we use our design process to help guide us. This is why one of the most important decisions for the COO to make before starting is deciding on a design process.

There are many design processes out there like IDEO's human-centered design process, The Engineering Design Process, or the Next Generation Science Standards. A science teacher might even adapt the scientific method into a design process, but the design process that works best for my EdCorps is the design thinking process developed by Stanford's d.school.

When I started planning how our EdCorps would work, I immersed myself in the d.school design process. I found d.school's focus on empathy to be a piece of the design process I wanted to expose my students to. What makes the d.school design process special is its focus on empathy throughout the process. The easiest way to think about the d.school design process is project-based learning + empathy = Design Thinking. Kevin Jarrett, educator and design thinking expert, put the importance of empathy in design like this: "The addition of empathy to the design process is key. Design Thinking gives the designer a user to design for throughout the process. For example, it is one thing to tell students to design a toaster, yet it is another thing to ask them to design a way to heat food up quickly for people on the go. The addition of empathy in the process is central and key. Otherwise, it's just regular old design, like "design me a toaster." Ok. Easy enough. Think about it, though; the entire process could take place without any significant user interaction. Design a way to heat food quickly for people on the go is user-focused on the needs, and a toaster might not be what's developed. That's the problem with design in K-12 up to now; it's all just process. It doesn't make it worthless; it just makes it NOT design thinking because there's no empathy. By using a design process that focuses on empathy, I can get cross-curricular in class in the most important way: I can challenge my students' preconceived notions of other people and their problems. By using a design process that challenges students to walk in someone else's shoes to better understand them and the problems they face has been the best part of running an EdCorp.

I've made two changes to d.school's design thinking process. I modified the process to include more interaction between students and the people they're trying to help, and I simplified their design thinking process for middle school students. D.school's design thinking process is totally open-sourced, so don't be afraid to check it out and come up with a process that meets your needs.

Our design process has five stages: Empathize, Define, Imagine, Make, and Test. Each has its own key activities for students to work through.

Stage 1: Empathy

Teachers: Grant Knowles & Kaitlin Melda
EdCorps: Lightning Orthotics
Location: Chattanooga, Tennessee

Grant Knowles: I'd used entrepreneurship as a vehicle for learning in my sixth-grade language arts class. Students learned about the language arts standards by finding needs in the community, determining the causes and effects, and creating theoretical social entrepreneurships, which culminated in a "Shark Tank"-style live pitch to "sharks" from the community. I loved the theory, but never put things into practice until meeting the Real World Scholars crew at the Pitt Fab Institute in 2017. I saw that I wasn't alone; rather, I was surrounded by educators already moving full speed. I was blown away, inspired, and ready to go all-in. What's happened since diving in has been the most authentic, empowering learning experience that I've witnessed.

To be organic, I need help sharing our story, so let me introduce you to Kaitlyn Melda, our Director of Operations, and one of the best humans I know. She'll help tell this story.

Kaitlyn Melda: We held a contest at the beginning of the year. The goal of the contest was to 3D print something that would help others. One of the groups printed an orthotic, an artificial support for limbs or the spine.

The next day we held a bunch of empathy challenges. We had to try to brush our teeth without our fingers and type using only one finger. It was a challenge. We were all struggling to do everything we were expected to do that day. Most of us were confused about how someone could do all that on a daily basis. Later that week, we had someone from Siskin Rehabilitation Center come in and answer all of our questions. He talked about the causes of some of the injuries and of how much orthotics costs. We were stunned by how expensive it was for an orthotic, even if the patient had insurance. None of us knew what we were doing, but we did know we wanted to continue to help.

We began coming up with ideas for orthotics we could sell. Some of these included the universal bottle opener, the cutlery adapter, and the pen adapter. The goal for us was to sell orthotics for a low price to people who needed them.

Grant: Kaitlyn brings up a crucial point—NONE of us knew what we were doing. I was scared. There's no way around that. I'm very comfortable taking risks, and I thought we were taking an appropriate risk trying to develop our knowledge, skills, and habits through starting a business. Now, one emotional conversation with a physical therapist later, and I've got a classroom full of sixth graders wanting to hack the medical industry. I was legitimately scared. I knew nothing about users' needs, nothing about how to make orthotic devices, and I felt like we would be in way over our heads. I had to remind myself that I've learned that the best learning happens when I get the heck out of the way, and just help the snowball get bigger and bigger as it rolls: we were officially an orthotics business. Well, in reality, we were a group of people who wanted to make orthotics, but not a business yet. The first steps came from talking to another EdCorp, The Upstander Brand, in Louisiana.

We had a conference with The Upstander Brand, and they told us how they organized their business. They had their business organized into departments: operations, communications, budget and finance, and promotions. We based our departments off of theirs. It was both fun and a challenge for me to make sure all the other departments were on task and doing what they needed to do. I knew the other students, too, were having a hard time starting somewhere.

Our first models were crude, but they gave us something to start testing. I've made plenty of mistakes in helping run the business, but one decision I made seemed to work well. We threw nothing out. Every prototype or iteration that didn't work or broke avoided the trash can, and instead ended up proudly hot glued to foam board and displayed in what became a mini-museum of sorts. What could have been seen negatively was something the students were (and are) incredibly proud of, and is a must-see tour stop whenever anyone comes into the lab. Their learning is visible. Their growth can easily be seen from across the room, and their pride is palpable. On the most challenging of days, seeing their resilience reminds us to keep pivoting and pushing forward.

We had a user named Mandy come in. She has a cervical vertebrae injury and lost the use of her hands and wrists. She said her biggest wish was to be able to eat steak in public without being embarrassed. We began giving her some of the products we made to try and help her. It was really awesome to have her give us feedback—she helped us realize things about our orthotics that we hadn't realized beforehand. Then we continued to fix the orthotics until they worked for her. It was a very ecstatic feeling when we heard she had gone to a restaurant and had gotten to eat steak by herself without being embarrassed. It is also crazy that not many kids get to go through the experiences we have. I was so happy to hear that one of our orthotics helped someone, but I also felt anxiety because we had so much more to do. I cannot tell you how many times we had to tweak or fix things. We had to move our dates back a lot because of the slight issues that messed up the product. I was stressed out by this because we had to start to sell our products, and with all these little tweaks, the date was pushed up further and further.

Kaitlyn: It was meeting people like Mandy and others that kept our tank filled. We went long stretches without big milestones or feelings of success, and sometimes I wondered if the students would just be done with it, but they never stopped. The students remained authentically engaged because they've found their "who." They knew who is affected by their learning, and they've stayed driven to help others. Lightning Orthotics wasn't done for a grade, so no one was pressing to get their A or just pass. So, when it came time to define our business model, I sat back and observed as the students presented the cost of each orthotic and then debated how to set prices. Others had done research and knew how much our possible competitors were charging for equivalent pieces. The students could set prices far above costs and still come in cheaper than their competitors, but that wasn't their decision. To a person, each student voted to keep prices as low as possible. They referred back to meeting with the physical therapist on that day we became Lightning Orthotics, and they remembered the *why*—we are Lightning Orthotics because we saw people in need, and knew we had the tools to help. We'll find revenue streams in other ways, and use the revenue to keep the business going, but all of those decisions will continue to be made by middle school students, and we're a better business for it.

Grant: As far as integrating our EdCorp into the curriculum, my most impactful classroom learning came from the basketball court this year, or rather, from standing on the side of it. "Lead loudly" was my most often used phrase in practice, before games, during games, and reflecting afterward. As a coach, my expectations are high on the court, in the classroom, in practice, and outside. I ask my team to grow as leaders, to model for each other, to be courageous, to be compassionate—and yet here I was, standing on the sideline, head throbbing as I am yelling out every rotation, every call, every read all while being outside the game, from the far end of the court. My head was hurting, and I wasn't helping. I called a timeout and implored my team to talk, and then it hit me: how can I expect them to talk if I don't stop talking? How can I expect them to grow as leaders if I don't give them room to grow?

Sitting and watching my team play was excruciating at first. I saw mistakes being made and wanted to jump up and help, but the team began to talk. They began to grow, and then grew quickly. They were able to grow because they had space. They were able to grow because they were able to make mistakes, and able to recover.

This learning came hard for me, but when it did it, it was applied in the classroom as well. Our EdCorp, Lightning Orthotics, had always been student-run, but so often I was making the reads about what was needed and then handing that over to them. How could I expect them to continue to grow if I was doing all of the need-finding? How could I call it their business if I was still doing the critical thinking for them?

So here goes something of a Lucky Seven (7) things I've learned in my first year running an EdCorps.

1. Growing leaders need room to grow.
Just about a year ago, I met Audrey, Elyse, and Michael from the Real World Scholars at the Pitt Fab Institute. Our school had recently been awarded a VWeLab, providing a digital fabrication space for our students to authentically create. I wasn't sure how that would best be leveraged, and then here comes this Elyse Burden, showing us video of herself falling off a stage, and sharing how she used to video herself polishing rocks, being vulnerable, being real, and offering an opportunity for my students to take action in using the space. What followed was a year full of the most powerful and transformative learning that my students and myself have experienced. This is an attempt to share some of what we learned as we started this business to help others. It's by no means comprehensive, and there is still an incredible amount of learning and work ahead of us, but there is power in being vulnerable and in sharing the learning as it is happening and still half-baked. Elyse and Margaret Atkinson have taught me that, and I've tried to learn it.

2. Trust is a gateway to everything.
We learned to move with the speed of intentionality, meaning that we wanted to sprint, but knew we had to be slow and intentional. We didn't make a sale. We didn't mean to; we didn't put our products up for market. I planned to sell small scale aquaponics, but the students had other, better ideas. They found a need, they found people in need, and they needed to help, but that meant we were a sixth-grade business looking to hack a medical industry -- getting things right is the only way we can go. Intentionality was our speed, but we couldn't get anywhere without trust. We wanted to rush forward, but we needed to know each other before we could get real work done. We

needed to know each other's stories, how to build on each other's strengths, and help push each other in areas of need. Trust allows us to communicate, to care, and to take risks, which takes me to number three.

3. We all have to separate self-doubt from idea-doubt.
To authentically ship your ideas, you've got to get them outside your comfort zone. This is next to impossible to do if you feel like you're putting your person out for judgment.

4. Done is better than perfect.
If we are being all vulnerable and trusting, then I can say that my competitive side is our biggest challenge. We got our first package out in May, just before school closed. We worked on it for months. The point of the package was to be a mock ship-ment, to assess ourselves, and to give feedback. I held that up. I wanted things to be perfect, but didn't that defeat the point? Done lets us receive authentic feedback. Done lets us learn and move, so striving for perfection slows our growth. Done allows us to rapidly prototype, and that lets us help others.

5. Treat the patient, not the problem.
The most important learning the students grew into this year was understanding that solving one challenge didn't become a solution for challenges. As we met with patients to define our challenge and receive feedback, we found ourselves working to help patients looking to get into wheelchair racing. Hard work and innovation led us to start iterating some possibilities that might help. We began designing FOR rather than WITH. We began trying to solve a problem rather than trying to help a person. What worked or looked like it might work for one person didn't work for others. It was a great reminder for us that design thinking is a mindset, not a map for us to check off. People are at the center of what we do. People are at the center of the process.

6. Agree on how you will disagree.

Conflict comes when people are passionate and take things personally. It's natural, it's going to happen, but it can be a positive driver. We've got a truly student-dreamed and student-run business, and that means there are times when we've got multiple, passionate opinions in any given moment. If we know that we're going to have differences, then we need to agree on how we will resolve them before we have them.

My mom, the wonderful woman that she is, gave me my love for board and card games. She was competitive, passionate, and had a knack for explaining rules after they had been "broken." Explaining rules after they've been "broken" leads to negative conflict.

So, while we've all got our cooler heads, let them prevail by deciding how they will handle conflict. Will it be a straight vote? A representative group of students? Rock, paper, scissors? Whatever it is, decide early and be candid on how disagreements will be solved. For us, we set clear expectations for respectful discourse and agreed that we would settle with each head of department casting a vote as a representative of their department. We'll reflect on that as we start back up next year. Maybe we'll build new procedures, but having this agreement worked for us. It beat my mom's method.

7. Self-care is important.

If you're reading this, especially to this point, you may want to do all the things. This is a work in progress, but I know to do all the things, to empathize with so many others, to take on all the problems, you run the tank close to empty. Remember to prioritize yourself, to keep finding ways to fill the tank, if for no other reason than to keep going.

———

GRANT'S STORY captures the importance of leading with empathy when running an EdCorp. His story highlights ways that we can use empathy to build a culture of caring within our business. Empathy that starts within an EdCorps makes it easier to lead with empathy when it comes to working with customers.

In the Empathy stage, students focus on understanding the story and needs of their users. Everything is run through our design process to make sure we keep our users in mind because improving someone's life is the goal. Turning a profit is just a bonus.

We learn about our users and their challenges through four key activities that can be done and repeated in an order: Interviewing, Observing, Role Playing, and Researching.

Step 1a: Interview

Interviewing is the main way we learn to understand the feelings and needs of our users. If we don't understand our users and their needs, we won't be able to come up with a perfect solution for their problem. If we can't solve their problem, they won't buy our product.

We use empathy interviews in two main ways: to find problems to solve or validate preconceived ideas.

When we don't have an idea for a product, we use interviews to get to know people in our community and the frustrations or challenges they're facing. Through these conversations, and through the empathy stage as a whole, we will try to notice areas where we may be able to help improve their lives. Because, as d.school points out, practicing noticing helps find the opportunities and needs that exist all around us hidden in plain sight.

Other times, students will have an idea before they even start our design process. When students have these preconceived ideas, I challenge them to use the design process to validate that they, in fact, have identified an idea that will help someone and improve their lives. This validation starts by finding the people who have the problem that they think their idea will solve and empathizing with them. During these interviews, students aren't allowed to discuss their preconceived ideas with their interviewees. When interviewing for Empathy, we aren't interested in talking to users about solutions; that comes in the test stage. In the Empathy stage, we want to focus on our user's feelings and needs.

Regardless of which way students approach their interview, preparation is the key to a good interview because Empathy interviewing is a crucial step. It requires skill, discipline, and a process—or it just becomes a conversation. Students may even want to observe, research, and roleplay before an interview to help them make sure they're asking the right questions. Whenever you or your students plan to conduct an interview, preparation will be the key to success.

Preparing for an interview

Over time, we've developed an interview preparation process and guide that works for us. Our prep sheet (see resources) helps students break down an interview into four parts.

1. Introduction, Purpose, then Build Rapport: Students introduce themselves and share the purpose of the interview, and then transition into broad questions they can ask to open the conversation and warm up the interviewee.

- What does your average day look like?
- How would you describe your job? How would your boss describe your job?
- Are you learning anything new?
- How would your kids/significant other describe you?
- What was the best/worst day you had…?
- What do you like to do for fun?
- What are some of the biggest challenges you currently face?

2. Dig for Stories and Talk about Feelings: In this section, students ask the user open-ended questions about the topic or problem, and then ask follow up-questions that result in the user telling stories and sharing their feelings about the topic or problem.

- Tell me about an experience...
- What are the best/worst parts about ...?
- Can you help me understand about ...?
- Walk me through how you . . . (made that decision, completed that task, got to a place, etc.).
- What were you thinking at that point?
- Why do you say that?
- Tell me more."
- How did you feel at that moment, when ____ happened?
- Could you tell me why that is important to you?
- What emotions do you have (about that)?

3. Clarify and Close: Students wrap up an interview by clarifying anything they still don't understand and ensure they understand why their problem is still a challenge. They end by thanking their user for their time and finding out when and how would be a good time for a follow-up.

- Why is this a problem?
- Have you ever tried to solve this problem?
- How many people does this problem affect?
- So, if I understand you correctly, you're saying...
- When did you realize this was a problem?
- Is there anything we didn't ask you that you wish we had?

Conducting the interview

Whether my students or I have arranged for the interview, we use our interview prep sheet to conduct the interview. No two interviews are the same, so we focus on best practices when conducting an interview to make the most of our time with our user:

- Record the interview, if possible. Audio is good. Video is better.
- Don't fill the silence. Allow pauses for your user to think and respond thoughtfully.
- Observe the way your user interacts with their environment (body language, tone, emotions, etc.).
- Ask "why?" often.

After an interview that has been recorded or during an interview that was unable to be recorded, students will focus on three areas of the interview to take notes on direct quotes, observations, and interesting or surprising things the interviewee said. Students will further unpack the interview later when they create an empathy map.

Step 1b: Observe

Observation is an empathy activity that asks students to watch their user interact with their problem in the real world. Students use our observation sheet (see resources) to focus on three key areas of observation: what they see, what they think, and what they feel while watching their user.

Students can record an observation and break it down later, or they can take notes while they're in the field. Either way, students are asked to answer the three questions about their user while they are observing them: What are they doing? How are they doing it? Why are they doing it that way? These three questions help students focus on concrete observations and helps them to be more empathetic by imagining what their user is experiencing on a thoughtful and emotional level.

To get the most out of observing during the Empathy stage, consider assigning a team member with no other responsibilities but to observe through the process.

Step 1c: Roleplay

Sometimes we know what problem we want to solve, but can't find a user to observe or interview. Other times, we may have interviewed and observed our users, but we don't really understand what they are going through. In both these instances, roleplay can be a great way to get students to walk in their user's shoes by *becoming* their user.

We do two versions of roleplaying. The first way we roleplay is by using our storyboard (see resources) to think through, sketch out, and then share what our user is going through when they interact with their problem.

The second, and better, way is to actually put yourself in your user's shoes and interact with their problem or frustration just like they do in real life. Living even a little bit of their experience will always trump imagining it. Whenever I can, I have students experience what their users experience. For example, when we worked with our local hospital to improve the phlebotomy process for kids, I arranged for the head of the department to come in and "take" students' blood. Minus the actual needle stick, students were put in the chair, swabbed with alcohol, and put through the phlebotomy process by the nurse. After, we had students role-play the kids having their blood drawn, the parents controlling their terrified child, and the nurse who has to draw the blood as the child thrashes about. Through this roleplay, students gained a new perspective for each person involved in the process. Undoubtedly, this new understanding of what's involved in the process allowed students to develop better solutions for improving the phle-botomy process.

Step 1d: Research

Intertwined with the other empathy activities as well as throughout the design process is our research activity. Students use our *Know. Want to know. Learned.* (KWL) research sheet (see resources) to help guide them as they try to find answers to questions that come up during the empathy stage. In the first column, students write everything they currently know about their topic. In the second column, they write down the questions they want to answer. The more specific the questions, the more likely they are to be successful. In the last column, students write down what they learned after doing your research. The KWL method works well, even in middle school and high school, and is a great place to start your journey if you are familiar with Project-based learning (PBL) since the KWL sheet lends itself well to the inquiry questions and research needed to launch a traditional PBL project.

The KWL research sheet is one of the only sheets I require to be online. I expect students to hyperlink the information on the sheet back to its original source.

Step 2: Empathy Map

After completing Empathy activities, students must have a thoughtful conversation around what they've experienced so they can continue to understand their user and their needs. Our favorite way to unpack learnings from the Empathy stage is our empathy map (see resources). There are a lot of different types of empathy maps, but they are similar in that they are a graphic organizer that asks students to recall and discuss what they learned in the empathy. Our empathy map consists of four quadrants: Challenges, Sound Bites, Interesting Stories, and Remaining Questions.

When it is time to empathy map, students gather their team and any artifacts from the empathy stage such as videos, audio, research, and notes. The goal of empathy mapping is to dive deep into their experiences and find insights, an accurate and deep intuitive understanding of a person, and opportunities to improve the life of their user.

The empathy map helps students make sense of their empathy activities so they can find insights and opportunities. In the Challenges quadrant, students are asked to discuss, reflect, and write about what challenges their user faced. Then, they're asked to think about why that problem is a problem for their user.

In the Sound Bites quadrant, students discuss memorable or surprising quotes that their user may have said. By unpacking these direct quotes, students can learn a lot about a user's thoughts and feelings.

As I mentioned, a good Empathy interview should prompt the interviewee to tell stories. As students reflect on the stories they've heard, they're encouraged to dissect and analyze stories in an attempt to gain insights into their user's thoughts and feelings as well as validate whether or not their solution will help their users.

The last quadrant on our empathy map asks students to jot down remaining questions that they have not only from their Empathy stage activities, but also questions they may have had while filling out their empathy map. Often, the empathy map will lead students to dive back into the Empathy stage. The remaining questions quadrant gives students a jump-off point for their next round of research, interviews, roleplays, or observations.

Stage 2: Define

Once students leave the Empathy stage, they take what they have learned about their user and their needs to the Define stage. The Define stage is an integral part of the design process where students will craft a meaningful and actionable problem statement, called a How Might We (HMW) question that they will focus on solving.[1]

Creating a HMW question starts with students developing their point-of-view (POV). A student's POV is what they believe their user's needs to be. Students use the POV to HMW graphic organizer (see resources), which is a modified version of the Interaction Design Foundation graphic organizer, to flesh out their POV. To do this, they just need to fill in the blanks:

A _____needs _____
       (user)   (user's need)

because _____.
                                   (Insight)

Here is my favorite point-of-view from this past year:

A <u>tech-phobic grandmother</u> needs <u>an easy way to remember to take her medicine</u> because <u>she doesn't have anyone to remind her.</u>

I love this POV because it uses a meaningful adjective to describe the user, clearly defines what she needs, and has a compelling insight. The insight could have read <u>because she forgets to take her medicine,</u> but because of the work done in the empathy stage, students realized that she forgets to take her medicine because she doesn't have anyone to remind her. This fact, which students found by digging deeper into her needs, will make for a more meaningful How Might We (HMW) question.

How Might We questions are questions that students will brainstorm around in the Imagine stage. Students can turn a POV to an HMW by changing their POV and focusing the scope of the question on being something that they can work around. An HMW question that is too broad likely won't be solvable for students where an HMW question that is too narrow might not generate enough to brainstorm around. To help students turn their POV into an appropriate HMW, I like to have them fill in the blanks again:

How might we _____ ... (action)

_____ ... (do what?)

for _____ ... (user)

In order to _____? (change what?)

Taking our above POV, students broadened the scope of the question to include all tech-phobic grandmothers who may benefit from a solution to the problem, and narrowed down the questions to include a specific reason they had no one to remind them. The How Might We question now reads:

How might we create an easy way for tech-phobic elderly people with no nearby relatives to remember to take their medicine to ensure they stay healthy?

This new How Might We question can now be carried forward to the Imagine stage, where students can brainstorm possible solutions.

Stage 3: Imagine

The Imagine stage is where we brainstorm around our How Might We question to find two or three possible solutions to take with us into the make stage. The imagine stage consists of three activities.

1. Generating Ideas

Students start by using their How Might We question to brainstorm a large, diverse array of possible solutions to their user's problem. During this process, my students will follow best practices for generating ideas that I've adapted from the d.school method of brainstorming:

- *Don't hate on ideas, say 'Yes and…' instead*: while there are bad ideas, when generating ideas during a brainstorm is not the time to question them. It is important to stress to students that ideas will be judged in the next stage, as students tend to get stuck hating on ideas during this stage of design. Encourage students to build on ideas, even the bad ones, because you never know what will turn into a great idea.
- *One conversation about one idea at a time. Not too long.* Talking about one idea is important for group focus, but we don't want to spend too much time talking about the same idea. The group should feel out when the conversation about an idea is dying and move on to the next idea. The group can always circle back to an idea if they need to.
- *Add constraints to ideas when you're stuck.* Constraints are limitations on an idea. If students struggle to come up with ideas or the brainstorm begins to slow down, I encourage them to add

constraints. For example, if they have a high-tech idea, I'll encourage them to think of a low or no-tech idea. Constraints can keep a brainstorm going and can help generate new ideas.

2. Research Ideas

Between brainstorming ideas and selecting ideas, students will stop to do research to help refine their ideas. Good ideas, after research, may not be so good. Bad or impossible ideas can also find new life after research. Students use our KWL sheet (see resources) to keep track of what they already know about an idea (K), what they want to know (W), and what they learned by doing research (L). Research will help students make informed decisions during the idea selection process.

3. Selecting Ideas

We use compromise, voting, and our idea selection sheet (see resources) to select two or three possible solutions to bring to the make stage. It is important that students pick several ideas to move forward because building multiple prototypes at the same time is beneficial in a lot of ways (I'll discuss this further in the Test section). In conjunction with our selection sheet, students follow these best practices:

- *Use statements like "I think," "I feel," "I wish," "I wonder," and "What if…" statements when judging ideas.* When students judge ideas, I encourage them to use I statements to help keep group harmony since I statements have been shown to help people feel less defensive.
- *Only one conversation about one idea at a time. Not too long.* Again, we don't want to perseverate on one idea for too long.
- *Compromise then vote.* We define compromise as supporting an idea you can live with. Even if it is not their favorite idea, if they can live with it, students are encouraged to vote for an idea. In a vote, each team member gets three votes to spend on their three favorite ideas. Students then eliminate,

compromise, and vote again until they are left with two or three ideas.

Stage 4: Make

The make stage is where we turn ideas into prototypes. The first step in this stage is unique.

Step 1: Sketch and Pitch

When we first started out, I used to let students start building proto- types right away. This led to a lot of wasted time and resources because students didn't put in the thought they needed to build a useful proto- type. To slow students down and force them to think deeper about their prototypes, I created the Sketch and Pitch step. Using our Sketch and Pitch sheet (see resources) before they build anything physical, students must draw a detailed sketch for each idea and write a pitch on how it works. After they have a good Sketch and Pitch, I will then have them pitch the ideas to their users to find validation for their ideas using our feedback recording sheet (see resources). Having another point of contact with their user at the early prototype stage has led to more meaningful prototypes.

Step 2: Prototyping

After unpacking user feedback, students can start to build their first prototype. The key to prototyping is to build the most basic version of the prototype that can be tested by users. Prototypes should be built as quickly and cheaply as possible. We will often start with cardboard prototyping. Things like color and materials don't matter until later. What matters is function. Once students have a prototype that they can test with users, they'll need to fill out a test card.

Step 3: Test Card

A test card (see resources) is used to help students determine what a successful test looks like. Before I had students fill out test cards, they would come back from the test stage, unsure if their prototype was successful.

Stage 5: Test

Other than the Empathy stage, Testing is the most important part of the design process. This stage is where students will find out if all their thoughtfulness and effort has helped them develop the perfect solution for their user.

Having defined success with their test card, students will give their user their prototype to use. It is important that students don't explain to the user how the prototype works. The solution should be intuitive. Instead, students should use their feedback sheet (see resources) and observation sheet (see resources) to watch their user with their prototype.

Earlier, we talked about why students would want to test two prototypes at the same time in the early stages. Having these multiple prototypes pays off in the test stage. One of our favorite things to do is to have users use two different prototypes during the same test and then compare and contrast them for students. Comparing and contrasting early prototypes helps students take the best features of multiple prototypes and combine them into one prototype in future iterations.

Persist or Pivot?

After testing with a user, students must decide whether to persist or pivot by unpacking feedback from the test stage and using the test reflection sheet (see resources). To persist means that they had some success testing their prototype with their user, and they want to take their prototype to the next level by going back to the Make stage and improving it—creating version 2.0 if you will. This next iteration of their prototype should still follow the rules of being made quickly and cheaply as they move closer to a final product.

To pivot means that students didn't have success in the test stage. To pivot means to go back to a stage in the design process where they think they may have missed something and being again, armed with what they've already learned, to make better a better solution.

Whatever stage students find themselves after the test stage is okay. Design and its stages are a fluid process that can be visited and revisited as often as needed. As long as students keep their users in mind, they're sure to create successful product to launch a business around.

Key Activities Once You Have A Product to Sell

Once you have designed a product, you should begin to help students move their idea to the marketplace. To do this, I've developed a list of the key activities you should do once you have a product to sell. These activities are not in any particular order. Instead, your students should look over the opportunities and decide which activities would be the most beneficial for their business.

Consider putting these activities in a slideshow that students can look through and then determine the next best step for their business.

Write A Product Description

As a former English teacher, I love the way entrepreneurship helps students hone their writing and communication skills. Writing a product description is a great opportunity for students to flex their persuasive writing muscles. Create a product description to entice customers to buy their product–they can use this on their online website, at in-person selling events, and on various marketing materials.

Set a Price

Ask people to pay too much for a product or service, and they won't buy it. Ask them to pay too little and your profits suffer, or they may even think your product is of poor quality. Price setting is both an exercise in math and studying human behavior. Have students research their cost-of-goods sold, the market price for their product, and any competitor's pricing. Use this information to set a price. I tell students to aim for at least a 50% profit margin.

Further, many students, especially younger students, are enamored with the idea of sales. Whether it is a percentage off or a Buy One, Get One (BOGO) sale, it is valuable to have students spend time learning why businesses have sales and when and how sales should happen—if at all.

Name your Business and Product

Naming your business is one of the hardest parts of starting an EdCorp. Be it a product in FH Gizmos or their business in FH Leads, I have found two schools of thought have helped us name things: a name should either be self-explanatory or should be nonsensical. Either way, make sure domains and social media handles are available before committing. This will also ensure that you aren't encroaching on an existing business that has the same name.

Create your Business Mission Statement

Have students create a mission statement that defines your business and goals.

A mission statement is the short, formal summary of what your business does and stands for. Your class must work together to write the mission statement. While mission statements are customer-facing, meaning they are meant to be shared with potential customers, you'll want to post your mission statement in your classroom to help inspire and focus students. Here are the mission statements students and I crafted when we started our EdCorps:

FH Gizmos's Mission Statement

FH Gizmos is a student-run business where we go beyond worksheets to learn about entrepreneurship by selling the solutions to your everyday problems. At FH Gizmos, we're learning to sell and selling to make a difference. 25% of our profit goes to our student-run charity, FH Gives, through which we make a difference in our community by supporting the people and programs we care about. So, when you buy from FH Gizmos, not only do you help us learn better, but you also help us help others. Remember, at FH Gizmos, your problem is our project!

FH Grows's Mission Statement

FH Grows is a student-run business where we learn to be entrepreneurs and stewards of the environment while leveraging technology and the Internet of Things to help our gardens grow. We sell our produce online and in our student-run farmers market. When we're not working in the gardens, we are trying to solve the environmental problems of our future. Remember, when you buy from us, you grow learning!

FH Leads's Mission Statement

We are a student-run business incubator. We give back to our community by using our design process to help local businesses grow. FH Leads will be the competitive advantage local businesses can't wait to hire because they know when they hire us, they are getting the tireless dedication and next-level innovation needed to grow their business. From our clients, we will learn more about careers and improve our skills as we make a positive impact wherever we go.

Create your Project Roadmap

A Project Roadmap (see resources) – sometimes referred to as a Project Plan – is a list of the next tasks or jobs, broken down by time period, that need to be completed to reach your business goals. This activity helps students turn goals into actionable activities that can then be delegated to team members to complete. Keeping the Project Roadmap updated will help students stay focused on growing their business. After you create a Project Roadmap, update it often as your business grows.

Develop A Social Impact Strategy

Simon Sinek says, "People don't buy *what* you do. They buy *why* you do it."[2] Why not pair your product with a cause that you care about? An Impact Strategy allows students to figure out what they care about and how they want to support that cause. A Social Impact Strategy should be included in your mission statement, pitches, core values, advertising, and anywhere else you tell the story of your business.

How valuable can a social impact strategy be? I had two students form a bracelet company called Wave Designs. They sold simple, string bracelets. What made their bracelets fly off the shelves was their story. Both of these students loved to spend time during recess playing and socializing with students who have Autism. They decided to take this passion and use their bracelets business to raise money for Autism Speaks. Currently, their bracelets are in two retail stores in our town, and they've made over $500, 25% of which they donated to Autism Speaks. You can read more about Wave Designs in the Students in Action section.

Core Values

Core values form the attitude; they are the foundation upon which the members of a company make decisions, plan strategies, and interact with each other and their users. Core values reflect what is important to you and your students and are a great way to frame the rules of your classroom for your kids. Having three to five core values to help guide your decision making and student interaction will be a boon for your business. I recreate core values with students every year. Some core values we've embraced are:

- No Days Off
- Teamwork Makes the Dreamwork
- Lead with Empathy
- Above and Beyond
- Fail Fast
- Fail Forward

- Try, Try Again
- Done is Better than Perfect
- Ship It!

Create a Tagline

Nike's *Just Do It!*, McDonald's *I'm Lovin' It*, and even movies all make use of taglines. You will want to take your mission statement and distill it down to a tagline. A tagline is a catchy phrase that captures the essence of your business. It can be used on marketing materials and worked into pitches to hook an audience.

- *FH Gizmos: Your Problem Is Our Project.*
- *FH Grows: When You Buy from Us, You Grow Learning.*
- *FH Leads: We Are the Competitive Advantage*
- *FH Gives: You Get. We Give.*

Create a Business Model Canvas

Create a Business Model Canvas to better understand the moving parts of the business, keep things organized, and help your students solve complex problems and generate new ideas.

Normally, a traditional business would create a business plan. Business plans are a long, complex, and tend to gather dust once written. Thanks to the rise of startup culture, we can use something called a Business Model Canvas to accomplish most of the goals of a business plan in a more engaging way that actually aligns with the learning process.

A Business Model Canvas is a single-paged, visual chart of the main elements you would expect to find in a business. It describes things like what value you are offering (value proposition), how you will get that value to your customers (customer channels), what you need to make it happen (key resources), and how the money will work (cost + revenue). While there is a standard business model canvas made popular by startups, you can modify a business model canvas to capture whatever entrepreneurial elements you deem fit.

At the end of every week, we spend time reviewing our business model canvas and reflecting on what we have accomplished during the week. We update the canvas and talk about goals and next steps. Using the canvas at the end of the week has been more successful than starting the week updating it.

Define Your Brand

In order to market anything—a product, a person, an organization, or an idea—you first need to define your brand. Once you define your brand, you'll be able to create a foundation for all your marketing efforts and strategies. Your brand definition serves as your measuring stick when evaluating any, and all, marketing materials, from your logo to the color of your business cards (Lake, 2019).[3]

One of the best-branded student businesses I've had was my Fortnite Friday team. The Fortnite Friday team was a team out of my eighth-grade business incubator, FH Leads. When given the opportunity to create a business, these five students decided to create an event company that specializes in hosting Fortnite tournaments at local businesses. From their logo to their marketing to their events, they captured the feeling and excitement of being part of a Fortnite tournament. They brought in the colors, fonts, and characters from Fortnite and used them to get people excited to play in their tournaments. And it worked! The Fortnite Friday team brought in over $500 per event.

Another beautifully branded business was Luck for Pups. The Luck for Pups team ran their business for three years as part of my program. Their goal was to make a dog toy specifically designed for shelter dogs or dogs who were home alone for long periods. This toy would focus more on stimulating a dog's brain than physical activity. It took students a long time to make a dog toy, so as they were working on their product, they used social media to raise awareness of the needs of dogs in shelters. Their social media marketing rivaled some of the biggest companies out there. They settled on complementary colors, beautiful fonts, and partnered with popular dog accounts on Instagram to continually bring informative, entertaining posts to their followers.

Create a Style Guide

A style guide is a set of standards for the writing and design of your product and business. What colors will your company use? What font? How will you talk about yourselves? Style guide answers those questions and more as it helps you build your brand.

Do Competition Research

Staying competitive means knowing your competition. Have students find their competitors and research what they're doing and how they're doing it. Students can use what they learn during competition research to make sure their product stands out from other products on the market.

Identify your Target Market and Create Customer Segments

A target market is made up of the groups of people who would buy your product or service. While optimistic, not everyone can be your target market. You will do better by getting specific and strategic about who you think will be buying your product. These different groups that make up a target market are called customer segments.

For example, I had a group of girls trying to sell a game for kids called Play It Again. Play It Again is a card game that challenges students to combine traditional outdoor games with fun and exciting rules to get kids outside and playing again. Play It Again's target market would not only be kids, but also the parents of those kids since they are the ones most likely to buy the product or give their kids the money to buy the game. Where you reach your target market and how you talk to your customer segments is important. I tell my students that parents are on Facebook, kids are on Instagram, and professionals are on Twitter.

In the case of Play It Again, students created parent-centered advertisements for the game and posted it to Facebook. These Facebook ads focused on what a great gift Play It Again would make for kids and had call-to-actions such as "let's get kids playing outside again!"

On Instagram, the Play It Again team focused on creating kid-centered advertisements. These advertisements focused on explaining how the game worked and how much fun the game was to play with friends.

In both cases, the Play It Again team identified their target market, created customer segments, and made sure they delivered the right message to the right customer using the right channel.

Create an Elevator Pitch

Imagine you are on an elevator with a potential customer. You should be able to pitch your idea or business before the elevator reaches the floor where the customer gets off. You'll want to give this customer an elevator pitch. An elevator pitch is a short speech that informs the listener about your business and/or product. Have students create an elevator pitch that captures the interest of the listener in a short amount of time.

Pitch an Investor

Some ideas are so big that they can't be funded from the classroom. That's where investors come in. Like Shark Tank, find and pitch an investor who might be interested in funding your project. An investor can be anyone who might want to invest in your company.

Create an Advisory Board

Find experts in the industry to help guide you on the next steps of running your business and selling your product.

Creating an advisory board serves a two-fold purpose. The first is to create a pool of people, both locally and abroad, that you and your students can turn to if you have questions while running your EdCorp. The second is opportunity generation. I have students reach out to our local small business associations, businesses in town, and experts online through social media. We let them know what our EdCorps are all about and ask if they would like to be on our advisory board. Many of the experts we reach out to are so in love with the idea of an EdCorp, they not only join the board, but also recommend other experts or share resources that help take our EdCorp to the next level.

We've received money, free supplies, software, and services like printing just because we asked, and our advisory board believes in our mission.

Develop Team Roles

Identify who will be doing what as part of the business. Write a job description for each member of the team.

Packaging

Packaging helps sell your product. Create packaging that falls in line with your style guide. Bubble mailers, custom wrapping paper, and stickers can make for great, simple packaging options.

Build A Website

Build a website that lets people know about your product and business. Include things like your mission statement and core values on your website. Use WordPress, Wix, Weebly, or another platform to build your site.

Create Social Media Accounts

Create social media accounts to help market your product. Use your style guide to make sure that your social media accounts look similar to help build your brand and your marketing strategy to reach customers.

Advertise Using a Social Media Marketing Strategy

Get creative and find fun ways to reach your customers and get them excited to buy your product. Use your style guide to make sure your campaign represents your business and use the test card from the Design stage to set goals and to identify what success looks like for your marketing campaign.

Create a Flyer

Sometimes making a flyer to advertise your product or business is appropriate. Advertise your product or business with a flyer that can be hung on our business bulletin board or distributed around town. Make sure to research what makes a good flyer.

Create a Business Card

Besides having all of your contact information and social media handles, a business card can say a lot about your business. Create a business card that conforms to your style guide and helps to grow your business.

Thank You Notes

Create a thank-you note to include with orders when people buy your customers. Thank-you notes are great to put on the back of business cards, too.

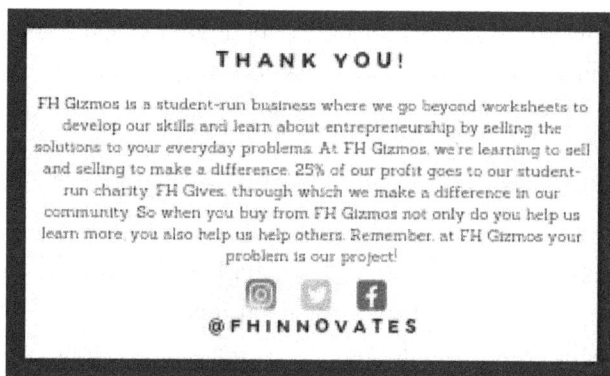

THANK YOU!

FH Gizmos is a student-run business where we go beyond worksheets to develop our skills and learn about entrepreneurship by selling the solutions to your everyday problems. At FH Gizmos, we're learning to sell and selling to make a difference. 25% of our profit goes to our student-run charity FH Gives, through which we make a difference in our community. So when you buy from FH Gizmos not only do you help us learn more, you also help us help others. Remember, at FH Gizmos your problem is our project!

@FHINNOVATES

Press Releases

A press release is an official announcement that your business can issue to the news media. You'll want to provide enough information so that news outlets have enough material for publishing their own stories about whatever your company is announcing in the press release.

Pitch a Local Business

Think your product would be a good fit to sell at a store in town? Pitch the store owner in person or via email about why they should sell your product in their store.

Get Feedback

There is never a bad time to get feedback. Get feedback from potential customers about your product, logo, packaging, press release, anything. Feedback is always useful and should be something you do early and often. Use our Feedback Recording sheet (See resources) to write down user feedback and our feedback reflection sheet to unpack what you learned from the feedback.

Minimize Expenses and Maximize Income

Find ways to lower your business expenses and maximize your income.

Create and Track Inventory

You never know when or how many orders you may get. You should have some inventory on-hand to sell. Keep track of your inventory in your Inventory Sheet. An inventory sheet will help you make sure you don't have too many products made that ties up your money, nor too few products that you would not be able to fill an order in a timely fashion.

Create a Pop-up Shop

Can you sell outside the basketball game? Can you sell at the town 5k? With a pop-up shop, you can sell anywhere. A pop-up shop is a temporary, physical 'shop' that can be set up anywhere. One of our favorite places to put on a pop-up shop is outside our local mall around Christmas. Work with school or community stakeholders to create a pop-up shop where you can sell your products! Pop-up shops should be flashy and eye-catching. You can use things like music, signage, and creative displays to draw people over to your pop-up shop.

Create a Ledger

Your ledger is the log of your day-to-day debits and credits. When you buy something—a debit, or make a sale—a credit, you need to update your ledger.

Create an Income Statement

The Income Statement is one of a company's core financial statements that shows its profit and loss over some time. The profit or loss is determined by taking all revenues and subtracting all expenses from both operating and non-operating activities.

Innovate and Iterate

Running a business is a mirror. It is a reflection of your hard work and effort. You should constantly be finding new ways to improve your product and grow your business. Once you've completed these activities, go back and do them again and again and again. You are never done when you run a business.

Key Activities When You've Made A Sale

Nothing is more exciting than making a sale. There are some obvious things to do when you make a sale, like package and ship your product. But there are also some less obvious pre-shipment and post-sale activities that every business should do as well.

Send a Confirmation Email

It may take a few days to get your product packaged and shipped. When you get an order, you should email your customer immediately and let them know you've received their order and will be shipping it shortly.

Include a Thank You Note and Business Card

Make sure to include your thank-you note and business card with your product.

Send an Invoice/Receipt

After a sale, it is good practice to give your customer proof that they purchased a product from you. The significant difference between the two is that the invoice is issued before the payment while the receipt is issued after the payment.

Update Your Ledger

Your ledger is the log of your day-to-day debits and credits. When you buy something, a debit, or make a sale, a credit, you need to update your Ledger.

Update Your Inventory Sheet

After a sale, update your Inventory Sheet. Make product or reorder supplies when you start to run low.

Update Your Income Statement

The Income Statement is one of a company's core financial statements that shows its profit and loss over some time. The profit or loss is determined by taking all revenues and subtracting all expenses from both operating and non-operating activities.

Check in With Customers

After the customer receives your product and periodically after, check in with them and tactfully include the following:

- A personal "thank you"
- Customer Satisfaction Survey
- An ask for use cases/testimonials
- An ask for referrals

Keep Them Cycling!

The important thing to stress to students throughout the design, marketing, sales, and finance cycles of running a business is that they are never done. They are only done for now and done is better than perfect. Remind them that entrepreneurship is a mirror. What they put into it is what they are going to get out of these cycles. When they finish a design, marketing campaign, or sale, they should dive back in to find ways to make their creations better.

Consider a mantra to help them keep cycling. "Done is better than perfect" is the mantra of our classroom. I say it all the time. Now my kids say it, too. It is our way of saying that what we do in our EdCorps is a process. We hurry up to get our products done so we can start our design process over again and make our products even better. By embracing the "done is better than perfect" mentality, I'm giving students permission to iterate. I am letting them know their first effort is not the only effort they'll be graded on because they can repeat our design process over and over again until they are happy with the results. By removing the stigma of perfection, my students are inspired to create again and again.

Chapter 5

ASSESSING LEARNING IN AN EDCORP

Teacher: Margret Atkinson
EdCorps: The Upstander Brand
School: Northwestern Middle School
Location: Zachary, Louisiana
Grade/Subject: Seventh & Eighth Grade English

The Old Meets the New
Old pedagogical paradigms can work in concert with the idea of the model of the Education Corporation. Although this might be a bold statement, it's entirely true. The way we teach students isolated skills that build on each other can work to complement how the entrepreneurial process and harnessing of potential and passion. In an English Language Arts classroom, nothing seems like a better fit than a chance for the students to read, research, and write about solutions to problems in their local and global communities. If, as educators, we must cultivate the whole child and prepare him or her for a world beyond the four walls of our classroom, we must have our eyes on both the content standards as well as other defining guides.

In "What are the 21st-century skills every student needs," published in 2016 by the World Economic Forum, there are sixteen skills listed for students in the 21st century. The three pillars of foundational skills (literacy, numeracy, financial, et al.), competencies (communication, collaboration, creativity, and critical thinking and problem solving), and character qualities (curiosity, leadership, social and cultural awareness, et al.) all point to a whole child. The author of the article, Jenny Soffel, even writes, "Combined with traditional skills, this social and emotional proficiency will equip students to succeed in the evolving digital economy." Our old paradigms of isolated skills or close readings of texts can only be strengthened through the life and vigor that is brought by a student-run business since its sole purpose is to have students working together to solve complex problems in their community.

Moreover, the International Society for Technology in Education (ISTE), a leader in the education field, has student standards that mirror that which the World Economic Forum advocates. They have seven standards (empowered learner, digital citizen, knowledge constructor, innovative designer, computational thinker, creative communicator, and global collaborator), and all of these point to what the EdCorp model can accomplish for students.

My students' EdCorp is The Upstander Brand, and its core mission is to engage, educate, and inspire others to be kind and find the Upstander in themselves. That mission is well served as we work to meet both ELA standards (reading, writing, critical analysis, speaking and listening, and intentional use of specific language) as well as ISTE standards and World Economic Forum research.

Building coalitions is paramount, so parents are always welcome in the classroom. Last year, a parent who is an entrepreneur visited the classroom to share his experience with starting his company and then held a short in-service for the budget department of the EdCorp. He spoke about the importance of collaboration and research for his medical company and said several times that the skills the students were learning as they worked in their respective departments of the Upstander Brand would mean that he could hire any of them when they started their own careers. This authentic feedback, from both a professional and an entrepreneur, affirmed the students' efforts and the vision behind the EdCorps model.

I do not take my responsibility lightly to my students, parents, administration, or district. And as an educator who believes in education's transformational power to create a better world, it can be understood that the World Economic Forum's research and advocacy, the Student Standards (2016) ISTE celebrates, and authentic feedback from local entrepreneurs all point to a reality: an EdCorp classroom can be housed within a larger academic content classroom, like an English Language Arts classroom.

Standards + Buy-in + Expectations
Traditional ELA standards cover reading (both literature and informational texts), writing, listening and speaking, and language. My students, then, can read and write for a variety of purposes, and we do. Concept development frames my curriculum, so any reading material is housed under the umbrella of each concept we are developing. Seventh grade develops power, structure, relationships, and exploration, while eighth grade develops patterns, force, respect, and order and chaos. Classics and seminal words gird the students' choices of literature, but I am also able to offer a global perspective to my students through novels like *The Long Walk to Water, Amal Unbound, The Red Pencil, I Am Malala,* and *A Long Way Gone,* as well as through informational texts provided by the United

Nations' Sustainable Development Goals (SDGs). We can critically read these works, develop concepts, and inform our greater understanding of a global community. This work builds to The Upstander Brand.

Our close readings, provided by the state and LearnZillion, as well as cold readings from Common Lit, play a part, too. A close reading of "A Brief History of the Salem Witch Trials" or Wordsworth's "I Wandered Lonely as a Cloud" informs our greater understanding and helps the students build critical skills that transfer to other works of literature. Through our discussions of text structure and character motivation, students engage in dialogue that creates a better understanding. All of this work builds to The Upstander Brand.

ISTE student standards remind my students that they are in an ELA classroom but need not to lose sight of standards held by others. The seven standards are in our classroom. They are on the poster from ISTE. And they are in practice, as they send an email to Lightning Orthotics, an EdCorp in Chattanooga. They are in practice as they interview a young woman refugee who escaped terror in South Sudan. And all of this work builds to The Upstander Brand.

Expectations for EdCorps follow many models, and the EdCorps around the country all have their distinctive personalities. As The Upstander Brand is housed in an ELA classroom, my students have expectations that align with traditional ELA expectations. We practice application of grammar, writing structure, MLA formatting for our research, and use of persuasive techniques. But there is another layer of expectations: National History Day (NHD). This national program engages students in historical research and allows them to present their greater thesis in one of five ways (website, exhibit board, documentary, paper, and performance). NHD has expectations for how the research is presented, and those expectations provide a framework for our EdCorp expectations. Just as my students create an annotated bibliography and process paper for their NHD projects, my students create an annotated bibliography and process paper for the EdCorp. All of this work builds to The Upstander Brand.

Between standards and expectations, my classroom has structure. With layers of student voice, student choice, classical literature, global perspectives, close and cold reads, Greek and Latin roots, emails, academic essays, NHD, and EdCorps, my classroom has fluidity and responsiveness. But there is no magic bullet for test success. Having robust instruction that allows students to practice the same skills in multiple ways, then, can be nothing but beneficial.

Engaging, Empowering, and Cultivating

All of this work builds to The Upstander Brand.

The Upstander Brand was established in 2016, with a grant from Real World Scholars. I have researched the Upstander (our definition is a person who makes a positive choice in times of crisis or conflict) since 2010, through formal grants given by The Holocaust and Jewish Resistance Teachers Program (HJRTP) and Fund for Teachers and informal study at museums. Although the Upstander initially only lived in the eighth-grade year when we studied the Holocaust and World War II, my at-the-time sixth grade and seventh grade heard whispers of the Upstander and insisted that we discuss Upstanders in other historical contexts. That was in 2013, and it was one of the most transformational moments for me of my professional career: my students craved ways to celebrate kindness and the humanity of others. I had never even thought to talk about Upstanders outside of the context of the Holocaust, and it was my students who reminded me that the Upstander is in all of us, all of the time, throughout all of history. The Upstander quickly became an integral part of our classroom culture, and so when Elyse, my students, and I had the fateful conference call in April of 2016, I knew serendipity was the only way to live life. Since The Upstander Brand's belief is to empower, educate, and inspire others to be Upstanders, the EdCorps itself needs to ensure that the students themselves are empowered, educated, and inspired. And to be clear, honoring global perspectives engages students. Finding passions engages students. Allowing students to "just go" empowers students. Suggesting collaboration space with other students and leaders in professional fields empowers students.

The Upstander Brand is divided into eight departments, from the operation department who helps manage tasks and the flow of the EdCorp, to the budget department, to the engineering department, to the music department (housed under the creative department), to the communications department, which is comprised of both public relations/marketing and partnerships (coordinating, via email, internal and external relationships). This is a work in progress, and the students know that everything is fluid. They self-select into departments (except operations), and they use their talents to support and even build out the structure of the EdCorp. We did not start with a music department, but after the current ninth graders (graduates of the business) came one day with lyrics and guitar chords for their new song, "One Little Act," we all knew it was time for a music department.

Eighth graders are the managers of the business, and seventh graders are their subordinates. This allows for leadership opportunities from both grades, as seventh graders are often instructed to follow the hierarchy if there is a concern or point of conflict. They have to solve their problems together. Managers can set tasks and coordinate with me. As seventh grade is their first year in the business, everything is new. After a work session last week about creating awareness for SDG6, clean water and sanitation, I overheard a seventh-grader tell her friends, "This was really fun." That same seventh-grader then asked me when we would have more time for the business. Isn't that what we aspire to as educators? Engagement, sense of self, and a desire to learn more?

I am far from being mechanically or numerically inclined, so even though I try to always let all of the students figure things out on their own, that experience is especially authentic for the budget and engineering department. In trying to set up our 3D printer, the eighth-grade engineering department is *almost* fully self-reliant. These boys, these football-playing-soccer-playing-right-brained-boys have given up their lunch socialization and spontaneously erupted into cheers each time they figure out the next step for the printer. From being flummoxed about the correct software to a conference call with Lightning Orthotics' engineering department, we are now a proud owner of a 3D printed cube. There will be more to come. I know it. I believe it.

Isn't that our ideal as educators? Empowerment, sense of self, and a desire to push through challenges?

Leadership in the Upstander Brand sometimes happens organically and without any cultivation on my part. A seventh-grade student, who often dismisses the need for writing and communication in general, volunteered to email our principal to ask permission for an idea the Creative Department had. We recently were honored to record a podcast with Jennifer Casa-Todd, author of *Social LEADia*. As eighth-graders were debriefing with seventh graders about the experience, one eighth-grader piped up and said, "Now listen, seventh grade, I see on your faces that you are disappointed you were not on the podcast. But you have to understand that you need to continue to have experiences before you can really communicate with a larger audience." It. Was. Brilliant. I didn't even see their faces because seventh grade's heads were turned to the eighth graders. All of it was totally organic on her part.

Isn't that what I always hoped for as an educator? Engagement, empowerment, a sense of self, and a desire to show the best versions of themselves.

In working together to serve something greater than themselves, they are empowered and engaged. That is never better seen than over our years raising money for charities, whether it is a national organization like the American Red Cross or a classroom in Houston, who was devastated by Hurricane Harvey. We sell bookmarks, wristbands, and stickers, all created to inspire others to be an Upstander. We sold baked goods and earned more than $900 to be able to donate to a classroom in Houston who suffered loss after Hurricane Harvey. My students had struggled with the flooding in Louisiana in 2016, and when Harvey hit in 2017, they immediately empathized and wanted to help. Suddenly, the school community became involved; students bought the baked goods, our cafeteria staff donated baked goods, and we were able to use that money on behalf of the school for good. Those experiences have given us the confidence to write press releases, create social media campaigns, and share our stories on a local news station multiple times. The public relations/marketing department are experts in creating posts for Twitter and Instagram as well as communicating on live television. The students are autonomous learners.

Isn't that what we plan for as educators? Cultivation, sense of self, and a desire to serve others.

This might feel different than a traditional ELA classroom, and it some ways, it is. We still read, write, and apply. We still build critical reading and analysis skills. We still take tests and have expectations.

But ultimately, having all of the experiences from The Upstander Brand while in an ELA classroom cultivates the whole child.

Your Student-Run Business: Authentic Community
Your classroom is a microcosm for the world.

It always has been, and it always will be.

What the students learn about themselves and others, about socialization and organization, about knowledge and how ideas build, about interpersonal and intrapersonal communication, is reiterated in the adult world.

So, allowing students to use content standards and technology standards in authentic ways creates an authentic community. These experiences will ingrain in them lessons, which will give the individual longitudinal success.

Believing in the power of the entrepreneurial learning process to transform education gives you the courage to dovetail traditional and visionary, expectations and ideals.

Keeping yourself responsive to moments of inspiration will help support that authentic community.

Building coalitions with your administration, district, parents, and students will build your authentic community.

Honoring others and remembering that the ultimate goal is to cultivate the child so that he or she will be affirmed for the potential that will change the world is exactly what our greatest gift to future will be.

Assessing students in an EdCorp is a delicate balance of grading the content you have to teach and assessing students on their skill development.

In my EdCorp, I focus on five key skills: problem-solving, teamwork, getting and using feedback, goal setting, and persistence.

Developing these skills requires authentic, hands-on experiences in a low-risk environment. Students can't develop a skill if they don't apply it, and students won't try to apply a skill if they think they will be punished for failure.

While students do the work and apply their skills, I use tight feedback loops and reflection activities to keep them learning and moving in the right direction.

———

Feedback Loops

The most important thing when assessing in an EdCorp is to create tight feedback loops. Because the design process and running a business are circular, students can keep going through the process over and over again to improve the quality of their product and business; feedback is what pushes students forward.

My feedback loops take three shapes: daily check-ins, performance reviews, and checkpoints.

Daily Check-In

I tell students it is easy to be successful in my class. All they have to do is set a goal. Meet the goal. Rinse. Repeat. Students start off the week by deciding what is the most pressing issue facing the business, then how and who is going to solve it. That becomes the goal. I encourage students to delegate work. If there are three members on the team, there should be three goals that they are working on individually. It doesn't take three people to design a flyer. Once they meet their goal, they brief their team and set a new goal for themselves. Students may meet many goals a day, or sometimes meeting their goal takes longer. As long as students are being productive, that is ok.

As the teacher, I keep it simple. I start class by spending a few minutes with every team, hearing their goals and the reasoning behind the goal setting. I give advice if they need it, and leave the team by writing down each team member's goal. Once I meet with every team, I start back at the beginning. The expectation when I return is that every team member has met their goals or made some progress toward it. That is it. So long as progress has been made during every loop I do in class, students are on track. I spend most days of the week looping through teams, keeping track of their goals, and giving feedback and advice. With an average of eight teams per class, I usually get through three or four check-ins per day.

Performance Review

While Daily Check-Ins cover the day-to-day operations of students' EdCorps, toward the end of the week, we have performance review. During performance review, students and I reflect on what went right and what went wrong during the week. With the focus being on holistic, big-picture social/emotional learning, I have performance questions I use to have a conversation with students around teamwork, goal setting, persistence, and how they used feedback to make improvements to themselves, team, or business.

Some questions include:

- How have you dealt with failure and bounced back from it?
- When you had extra time, how did you spend it?

- What help or advice were you given this week? Was it useful?
- Who helped you the most this week?
- Tell me about an idea you started that involved collaboration with your colleagues that improved the business.
- If you find yourself working with a team that is not motivated, how would you keep yourself motivated and motivate others?
- What do you hope to accomplish this coming week?
- What was your greatest accomplishment this week?

Not only do these questions help students better understand what it means to work as a unit and be entrepreneurs, but it also doubles as a form of interview preparation, which is great because many of my students will be getting their first jobs toward the end of my program.

Check Points

With the micro and macro aspects of running the business covered by Daily Check-Ins and Performance Review, I do everything I can to automate the activities of students when I am not with them. For example, there's a recording studio in our classroom. As you can imagine, it is a popular destination for many students. To keep things orderly, and to help students move forward in a design, students must complete certain checkpoints before they can use the recording studio. Whether making a podcast, commercial, or a video, students can't enter the recording studio without having a script, show notes, or a storyboard.

Another example is when students want to make a new product. The steps they need to take, the resources they need, and the materials they can use are all laid out for them. They only need to follow the steps I've created for them that represent best practices. When I come through for a daily check-in or call them over for performance review, they are expected to show their artifacts that would have been created should they have followed the steps. In the case of designing a product, an empathy map, brainstorming sheet, research, sketching, prototypes, testing card, and feedback sheets are artifacts that I would expect to see if they followed the checkpoints as laid out for them.

Just like a more traditional class uses scaffolding to break learning objectives into more manageable chunks, instituting a checkpoint system as a means to guide students through their design process while running an EdCorp is a great way to keep students moving forward toward a final product while keeping the focus on the process.

Chapter 6

STUDENTS IN ACTION

I've run versions of EdCorps for the last six years. One thing I've learned is that not every student is going to have the same experience in my classroom. This used to be my biggest fear: students going down many different paths, because I couldn't guarantee that each would have the same experience in my class. After a few years of running businesses with students, I realize that this is my program's biggest strength. Each student is walking their own, unique path during their time with me, determined by a combination of their effort, interactions with users, passion, resourcefulness, and opportunities. What they learn as they walk down that path is different, too. Every student will not have the same experience; they will have their own experience. And, ultimately, that is what I want for them: to leave my program having had an experience. It is through these experiences that real, relevant learning happens for my students. What better way to end then to let my students share what they did, why they did it, and what they learned? Here is the story of their journey, in their own words.

———

JMJ Frames

We walked into this class on the first day of school, not knowing what we were going to do. This was our first day of being sixth graders in a class new to us, FH Gizmos. When we were told to get with a group between two and three, we all looked and thought we would be an amazing group: Jack, Matt, and James.

We immediately started brainstorming an idea for what our business was going to be. The best thing we thought of was a video game, but as we watched videos on how to make a video game with Unity, it started off simple, but it progressively got harder, and we decided to pivot to a different project.

We came up with our new business idea, JMJ Frames, which stands for Jack, Matt, and James Frames. We were trying to solve the problem of picture frames being too plain. After talking to people who might want our frames, we decided to engrave picture frames using our very own laser cutter. The way we were going to make the picture frames amazing was to base the design around the school's logo with the school date at the bottom of the frames since parents said they would like a frame made specifically for school pictures.

Our business wants to succeed in what we are doing because the money we make supports our class. We want the future students in this class, FHGizmos, to have as much fun as we did. We plan to do this by putting all of our profit that we earned back into this class, so Mr. Aviles can fund projects like ours for other students.

One of our biggest problems was the ads that we made for Instagram and Facebook were not working out. They weren't resonating with our target market. Our business didn't have any business. We needed to fix that, so we decided to ask the owner of Coastal Decor, a local store in our town, if we could sell our frames in her store. She said yes! This was big for us because we had perfect timing. In two weeks, she was going to have a huge Christmas party. This was perfect for us because we had never sold a frame, and hopefully, many people would like our frame and purchase the frame at the party. We immediately got to work on our frame; we had to engrave it, stain it, and then make a sign to tell our story.

Our business had a great idea. We put our sign inside of the frame, so while people were looking at our frame, they could read the story about our business. The party was successful, which is what we were hoping for. We sold 7 frames for $20 each, which was amazing for us. After the party at Coastal Decor, we started to get a few sales online, which was a first for us. Our business was really starting to grow!

Once we had all these orders, we needed to fulfill them, which is not easy to do. First, we needed to engrave and stain all the frames, and then we needed to ship them.

As we come towards the end of the year, we have decided not to completely end our business. Our team has decided to put JMJ Frames on pause.

———

St. Jude's Supporters

Our team is Sydney, Gracyn, and Elsa, and we are all in sixth grade. Our original business was making metal engraved, beaded bracelets for $4.00. However, that didn't work, and if at first you don't succeed, try, try again.

Once we figured out that the metal engraving wouldn't work because our engraver couldn't cut through metal, we switched to leather. The leather we use gets custom engraved and cut by us, and thankfully, it looks even better than the metal would've. We now sell leather engraved, beaded bracelets for $4.00. 25% of our earnings, $1, go to St. Jude Research Hospital.

Our business reached out to a local bookstore, River Road Books, to see if they would sell our bracelets in their store. The answer was yes, and the owner wouldn't even take a cut in our sales. We are very happy the partnership worked out with River Road Books. Because of the risk we took with asking them, we made more money and reached more users. We sold a lot more bracelets because we asked River Road Books.

We also couldn't have chosen a better cause to donate to. The problem we were trying to solve was raising money for St. Jude, which runs solely on donations, which cannot be easy. We knew that it was a very good cause, so we donated as much as we could while also being able to run our business. At first, we thought it felt selfish not giving all our money to St. Jude, but we needed the other 75% to buy more materials so we could make more bracelets and in turn, donate more to St. Jude's. This is called social entrepreneurship. So, in a sense, all of the money was going to St. Jude.

We were trying to donate as much as we could because no family that goes to St. Jude has to pay a single medical bill—a bill for their stay, food, or any necessity. Everything is free, and that is amazing because not a lot of hospitals are not that considerate. St Jude really cares about its patients, and we wanted to thank them for that by helping them.

During our time in FH Gizmos, we learned a lot about how you can never stop growing your business and finding new ways to reach out to customers. We also learned that when you get stuck on something, you have to keep going and persisting. If we can't do something right the first time, then do it again differently or pivot. There are many ways you can help others, and we thought this may help save a child. We really did learn a lot about not only business, but also life skills in this class.

We attached a social impact piece to our business because we wanted to be able to donate to a cause that cares more about their patients than the money they are earning. Attaching a social impact piece to our business always gave us something to work for; we were doing something for somebody else, and it felt good. We were giving to lots of people in need. This also helped us set goals for ourselves when we got somewhat stuck in one spot. For example, sometimes during our class, it felt like we had done everything we possibly could have done for our business. Ads, social media, selling in-store, getting sales—but there is always something more to do. Our teacher has given us many examples. Examples about pitches, marketing, and what to do when you've made a product really helped us plan our next steps on our business roadmap. Our future plans for our business are to close down and maybe open back up next year, depending on whether or not we are in this class together again. If we are in this class again, we will be opening back up again, and of course, growing our business!

———

Wave Designs Bracelets

We're Brooke and Natalie. In September, we started our business, Wave Design Bracelets, making friendship bracelets and donating a portion of the profits to a cause that we cared about, Autism Speaks. Autism Speaks is an organization that helps out kids in need. Our business decided to sell bracelets in honor of our friends who have autism.

We had the idea to call a local boutique, Moon Child, and see if they would sell our bracelets. They said *yes,* and our business really took off. To keep up with all the orders, we hired Arthur, Brayden, and Owen to join our business as employees and help us make bracelets and get more things done. It was different, being in charge of three new team members, but we adjusted to the changes as quickly as we could and were able to make our many shipments to Moon Child over the semester. The owner, Jen, would ask for 50 bracelets a shipment. With our new teammates, it took us about a week to make all those bracelets. Half of the bracelets we made were blue for Autism awareness, and the other half of bracelets were other colors. We sold our bracelets for three dollars, with one dollar going to Autism Speaks.

During our time in class, we learned about working on a deadline and learned that we need to stay focused on getting work done. We were faced with problems like making enough bracelets in time, staying on top of the business portion of everything, like marketing and finance, besides production. We were taught the importance of working as a group and cooperating with others. Since we had a big group, it was key that we all worked together so that we could get things done. We also learned about how to attach a social impact on our business. We wanted to choose a charity that we all felt was impactful. This helped our business grow because people who bought our bracelets empathized with our feelings of wanting to help kids with autism. This social impact helped our bracelets sell, too. We had a sign in Moon Child with our story on it. It said how we were students and that we started this business to help Autism Speaks. People really liked our story.

One of the problems in our business was staying focused. We learned to overcome that problem by using our business canvas and roadmap to make sure we always had something to do, which was mostly making bracelets. Mr. Aviles' performance review also helped us keep on track and stay on task so that we would get everything we needed to get done. We made sure that we were organized with our plans for each day, and everybody was constantly working on a key activity.

Another problem we had was teaching our team how to make bracelets. Some of the team members had a hard time learning how to make the bracelets. It took time out of our class to teach our new team members how to make bracelets. Making the bracelets was sometimes difficult, but we powered through and continued working. It took a little long to get everyone making bracelets at a good pace so that we could have enough for Moon Child. Eventually, everyone was able to make at least one bracelet a class.

Our plans for our business in the future are to sell in new stores. One of the stores we reached out to is called Natural Elements. We gave them a call, and they said they would love our bracelets. We can't wait to deliver our bracelets to Natural Elements.

During the year, we got more comfortable making bracelets, and we all got closer as a team. As the year comes to an end, we hope that next year we can continue Wave Designs. When the semester was coming to an end, we wrote a thank-you letter to Moon Child and sent the check to Autism Speaks for the money that we raised to them. It was nice to see our hard work from the year pay off, and it felt good to know that we made a difference.

———

Skype Kids

We're Will, Jack, and Donovan, and we consulted for Skype in the Classroom. On the first day of FH Gizmos, Mr. Aviles asked us what problem we wanted to solve. We thought to work with Skype, who was looking for help, would be cool. The next week we had our first talk with Ross Smith. Ross is one of the people in charge of Skype in the Classroom. He told us he needed help coming up with ideas for a game that can be played over Skype between classrooms all over the world.

We initially thought the game would be a little bit like Jeopardy, but we then realized it would be too much like the actual game Jeopardy and it wouldn't be fun to students. The biggest problem is that it would be hard to use Skype with it. We decided to think of a better idea and thought of what we now call Skype Bowl, a quiz game in which you have to be the first one to answer math, science, or vocabulary questions to gain points. We were going to make the game on Skype in the Classroom and have classrooms Skyping other classrooms. Students Skyping other students. Not only would it promote Skype, but it would also be a fun way to learn from each other.

During the empathy stage, we Skyped a third-grade classroom for what they thought of Skype. The teacher and students said they were very happy about their experience with Skype. The only problem it sounded like there was that it could be hard to set up sometimes. Our user said she mostly used Skype for learning. For example, she was Skyping an author last year when they were in their nonfiction unit. She said it really helped them get tips on writing. Also, some kids in her class had connections to NASA, so they Skyped them when they were in a Solar System unit. It sounded like it really helped her in teaching. She lastly said that instead of traveling to meetings that are far away, she can just Skype them.

This feedback helped us sculpt our game. After that, we Skyped Ross again. We told him what the third-grade teacher said, and he told us to start working out details of the game and to make sure we incorporated what we learned from talking to users. We did just that. We remembered that to make this game worldwide, we have to remember that different classrooms have different time zones. We went on different sites to figure out how different time zones worked. Next, Mr. Aviles told us that in three weeks, we could go to the FH Gizmos selling event at a local shopping mall, the Grove, and find users to test our game. We immediately got to work on questions for Skype Bowl. We did this because we wanted to make sure the game would be successful when it came out. About a week before the Grove, we realized that we were not going to have an internet connection. We decided we needed to make a version of the game that could be played without the internet for testing. The people really liked our game. One person said, make sure that if you get it wrong, the robot host tells you why. Something to add was that the robot host has different avatars, different languages, genders, and personality, so everyone feels included during the game.

A few days after the Grove, we emailed Ross and told him about the feedback we got. Ross was happy and helped us start to make our robot host for Skype. To do that, we started to familiarize ourselves with Microsoft Azure because that is the program the interns from Skype's Ireland office, who Ross arranged to help us, were going to use to help us make our robot host for Skype Bowl. We wanted the host bot to be the host for every game, keep score, see if the questions are correct, and be the overall friendly host. We went on Microsoft Azure, and we figured out how it works. I actually started making a robot, and it was surprisingly easy! All you have to do is type in the name of the bot and all of the other information, and then test it out, and it answers on Skype.

The next step would be to program the bot to make it say what we want it to say. The last thing we did is packed up our business and closed it out. We have had a great time making this, and I am really happy that we picked this project. If I could rate this project, I would say that it is one million percent the best project I have ever done—from the beginning where we weren't even sure this was going to work, to now, when we are constructing a robot for the game we learned a lot.

We look forward to continuing this project next year.

————

Dollars for Dogs

We are Lilee, Molly, and Sylvie, and our business is Dollars for Dogs. We all decided that we want to help dogs in shelters. Our problem that we were trying to solve was that dogs in shelters need more love and support. We chose to solve this problem because we all adore dogs. We used the empathy stage to learn about what dogs are going through. We looked at pictures of less fortunate dogs, and it broke our hearts, and that's when we knew we needed to help. Molly came up with the idea of incorporating a charity into our business to help with our mission. We did some research and found that the Monmouth County SPCA was located close to us, and they are not a kill shelter. We reached out to them, and they agreed to partner with us.

Now that we had a social impact, we knew we had to come up with a product related to dogs. Using our design process and talking to dog owners, we soon came up with custom engraved dog tags for our product. This final idea was not very easy to come up with. We started out with rubber wristbands or bracelets to raise money for Monmouth SPCA, but that did not work out. The websites and businesses we tried to use were way too expensive and complicated. We had to make a pivot and come up with a different idea. After we had our next idea (dog tags), we started our business. We worked on marketing using things like flyers, business cards, pitches, and unique designs for our dog tags.

We started out not having enough sales. We were struggling, and we needed a helping boost. Soon, we heard the news that we were going to the Grove to sell. This was a huge helping hand for us. We sold a lot of tags, and we received many donations, and a lot of people took our flyers and ordered online after the Grove. We were allowed to stand outside and pitch to anyone who walked by. It was hard work, but we are glad we did it. We learned a lot about sales pitching there. The Grove was our favorite experience. We hoped to accomplish a donation of $20 by the end of the semester. By the end of the semester, we had accomplished our goal. We have already sold about $120, so the Monmouth County SPCA will get about $50. This goal took our time and effort and are proud of what we did.

Our team learned in class that we sometimes need to pivot. We also learned a lot about marketing and how to find our number one customers. I will definitely use this knowledge throughout my life. During our business, we made an Instagram account. We made this because we wanted to spread the word of our business. We also made this because mostly kids go on Instagram. Kids are not our best buyers, but they tell their parents about our business.

Our future plans for our business are to close it down until the next school year. We loved doing our business, but we decided that it would be too hard to do in between classes. We loved our business, and we hope that we made our customers happy. We especially hoped we helped shelter dogs with our donation. When we donate this money, it helps animals in need. It helps dogs get their meals, and it helps them in getting adopted. Every dollar counts. Most importantly, it helps keep dogs alive, so the next time you think about buying something special for your pet, think about the dogs in need.

Esports for Edu

Our team is Alex, Kole, and Alec. Our business is Esports for Edu. Our mission is to help other schools start esports teams, like our own, in a fun and friendly environment.

We started by creating documents with Mr. Aviles about how to start an esports team. Next, we made our logo, style guide, and presentation for educators interested in starting an esports team. We came up with a marketing plan to spread the word of our business. We also started to share the story of the FH Knights, our first of its kind middle school esports team, in hopes of inspiring others to get involved in esports. Sharing our story worked great. We were featured on ABC and PBS and did a lot of interviews.

Our esports team is currently playing Rocket League. Rocket League is a game where cars play soccer. However, this fast-paced car game isn't only about driving, but also about teamwork. We have been practicing hard. We have our practices on Mondays and Wednesdays during lunch and recess. At our practices, we practice rotations, communication, and strategy. We also top off our skills and have lots of fun. We are also helped by the player-coaches on the Rutgers University esports team and our coach, Mr. Aviles. Rutgers has one of the best college esports teams, and we even played their esports team because it has been hard to find other middle schools to play.

We did eventually find another middle school to play. We played the first-ever middle school esports match in history against William Annin Middle School (WAMS).

We started the best of four matches with WAMS with a win. Then me and Kole played the second match and lost. The seventh graders played their match and got crushed by the WAMS team. In the last match, the best two teams played the final match. The match lasted a long time, eventually going into overtime. Then we finally scored the winning goal. We tied with WAMS 2-2. After the match with WAMS, we celebrated our first match with a pizza party at a local pizza place. We had lots of fun playing, and our parents and friends watched; all of our practicing finally paying off. We will play WAMS again for a tiebreaker about a month from now. When we play next time, we will have our jerseys. How does this affect our business?

Being part of the esports team helps us know what we need to teach users to start their own esports team. We can help schools start an esports team from getting started, to running a practice, to joining big tournaments, having a support staff, and playing big games.

We learned how to start and run a business from the FH Gizmos program. We also learned how to advertise, and we also learned many other useful business skills, such as handling money, marketing, and selling. These skills will help me and my team thrive in the real world when we get older and bring our ideas to the next level. We also learned how to compromise with other group members, so we all could get what we wanted.

In the future, we hope to expand our business not just to the United States but to the world. We already helped start our school's own esports team, so we're ready to make esports for edu a household name. The story of our business doesn't end here. Next semester, our friend and teammate, Devin, will take over the business and continue our work. And after that, we will continue our business into the summer and then seventh grade and eighth grade, and maybe even high school. We also plan on continuing the esports team for the rest of the school year and into the next year!

Warrior Wear

We have created a business called Warrior Wear. Our class was challenged to create a business that would help others in need. We chose to help the Wounded Warrior Project because we wanted a way to show we care about our troops, like Isabella's father, who was in the military. We learned that not a lot of soldiers were able to get the help that they needed. We know that the Wounded Warrior Project is a trusted charity and thought it would be our best way to go.

We helped raise money for the Wounded Warrior Project by creating a survival bracelet company, Warrior Wear. We wanted to use a type of material that would be something that was related to the military and also strong enough that it won't break, so we created our bracelets from paracord. We decided to use paracord because it is commonly used in the military. For example, we know that when the Air Force soldiers jump out of planes, the parachute they use includes paracord. We used all different colors of paracord that are related to the branches of the military. We had blue and gray for the Navy, red and yellow for the Marines, and black and gold for the Army, and more. We also used purple for the middle color of the bracelet because that color is the color that represents all military branches. Our bracelets also used clips that have flint and steel, a whistle, and a mini compass on it. This bracelet is great for camping and wilderness survival and really feels like a military bracelet, which is why we wanted to add these cool features. To make the bracelets, we measured the user's wrist and divided that by two. That is how much we needed for each color. Then we braided it to the clip and finished it with a blob of hot glue. It took about 20 to 30 minutes to create each bracelet, and we put in all our hard work and effort.

Our goal was to raise at least $80 and donate 25% to the Wounded Warrior Project. We accomplished our goal and impacted soldiers by helping them with their health and family.

In our class, we learned to create a business, manage money, about time, and also to make sure our customers were satisfied. In class, we learned how to overcome obstacles. We were able to time everything as well as we could so we could have a well-organized business and still have time to create the best product we could put out.

We hope to improve our business by finding cool new ways to style our bracelets. We would like to use more colors and add more buckles to the bracelets, so all four sides have a buckle, and have all five colors on the bracelet in some way. Our future plans for this business are to keep making bracelets and helping Wounded Warriors. We hope to make our bracelets a bit cleaner when we come close to the end of the bracelet. We also hope that we can make our bracelets in other designs to expand the business. We would like to expand our business by making more products and getting our name out there, too, so that more people know about Warrior Wear.

Volunteerer

Hello, and welcome to our Volunteerer app that we made from scratch on MIT App Inventor. We worked on this app for a long time. Our team is made of two people, Austin and Bobby.

Our business, Volunteerer, is an app that allows people to set up events that others can volunteer for. We are trying to make it more accessible for people to volunteer for events. We decided to create this app because I noticed that my mother, the president of the Fair Haven PTA, says that it is hard for her to get people to volunteer for public events.

We decided we could solve this by creating an app that makes it easy for people to volunteer for things like school events. I think we have a great app that a lot of people will use. We know that the PTA would be able to use this without having to pay a lot of money because we asked about pricing. We plan to charge $1.99 for each event that you create, or you can buy a subscription for $6.99 that you can pay for each month. Our competitors cost almost $100 for the first month. We are providing a less costly, more understandable app.

We are still in the testing and changing stage of making the app. We are going to start a trail in Fair Haven, and then we might move it out to different towns (Little Silver, Red Bank, Rumson, Sea Bright, Middletown, etc.).

During our time in class, we have learned to code, which is a good skill to have, and we have learned about owning a business and how hard it can be. In the beginning, we had to figure out how to code. We used several YouTube videos to help us set up some of our screens, such as our login and sign up. One time, when we were working on our login screen, we accidentally deleted a component that was important, and that caused several weeks of trying to figure out what we did wrong. Eventually, we fixed this issue by rewatching the video and retracing our steps. Coding was also tedious at times. Sometimes, when we would get burned out from coding, we would take a break by helping other groups test their prototypes.

Our future plans for this are to continue into seventh and eighth grade and then possibly into high school. I think that this is a good business that we could continue with and make a lot of money.

Our journey of creating our volunteering app was very hard but also a very good learning experience.

———

Simply Beauty Box

Hello! We are the owners of Simply Beauty Box, Janie, Julia, and Anna! Our business is a subscription makeup box filled with age-appropriate makeup for girls our age. The problem that inspired this idea was that we thought about all the girls that we know that didn't know how to put on age-appropriate makeup and maybe even steal their mom's makeup. But, with our product, you know what to do, and there is the right, appropriate makeup for our age.

We wanted to make sure that everything was going to be appropriate for school, so we tested it out on users. After testing, we decided to include concealer, lip gloss, clear mascara, brow gel, and translucent powder and a powder brush in each box.

After we made sure everything was perfect, we started to film our videos. In order to learn to use these products correctly, users can follow our YouTube channel, where they can find multiple makeup tutorials on how to use the makeup in the box. On our channel, we have fun challenges, informational videos, and bloopers. We post at least once a week and maybe even two times! The videos go really in-depth about how to apply and use all of the makeup in the box. Later on, we want to get a QR scanner, so when someone gets their Simply Beauty Box, they will be able to watch our videos right away. We really enjoy our YouTube channel because it helps promote the business and is fun.

During our time in class, we realized that it takes a long time to start a business. You have to go through many different ideas, and also, when you think you have a GREAT idea, you have to rethink it. We had so many different ideas that could have been great, but we knew that we couldn't use them because it wasn't the right solution to our problem. We also realized that it takes a long time to get our products. The biggest struggle that we had was when we were making our videos. They took so long to make, and then we had to edit them.

One unique problem our business faced was finding funding. The boxes were too expensive for Mr. Aviles to fund, so we pitched people on our idea and asked them to invest in Simply Beauty Box. We raised over $100 and were able to buy our supplies with the money we raised.

We are planning to continue the business during seventh and eighth grade so we can keep selling the boxes to girls that don't know how to put makeup on. One day this business could be really big for girls 9-13. Soon, if more people buy our box, then we will move from our bubble mailer packaging to a real box. And if people buy the makeup in the new boxes, we could also maybe get higher-end brands. We also soon hope to become like the higher-end makeup subscription box brands.

Overall, we learned how to run a business, but most of all learned the value of friendship and how developing a good friendship makes your business run smoothly. When working together, you can get anything done. As the semester progressed, so did our relationship with each other. That was the highlight of running this business!

———

Simple Spray

Hi, we are Knollwood classmates, Amelia and Ava. In FH Gizmos, we had an assignment to make a problem into a solution. Our problem was stopping tick-borne diseases. We were inspired to make our product, The Simple Spray, because of Amelia's sister Emma. Emma was diagnosed with Lyme disease when she was 15.

When we first came to class, we used our design process to figure out how to solve the tick and flea disease problem. Solving a problem is harder than you think. We started off a little rough. We were going to make a wilderness kit, a tick kit, and even thought about making a bandage that comes with a solution – but our problem was harder than that. We finally landed on a spray to help prevent ticks from getting on you when you're out in the woods.

We did a lot of research and talked to a lot of people and eventually came up with The Simple Spray. The Simple Spray is made with all-natural fragrances and essential oils. It includes citronella, witch hazel, sweet lemongrass, lavender, and rose geranium. In our research, we read studies that showed these oils have been shown to keep ticks and fleas away.

We were going to be putting our product in Canyon Pass, a local outdoors store, in the spring. The day we went to present our story and product with Canyon Pass, we were nervous but prepared. We thought it would be different than it went, but we were brave enough to make a successful sale. This inspired us to keep going since we are doing this for a cause. We would like to donate some of the money to Global Lyme Alliance when we start to make sales. With our product at Canyon Pass, we will be including pamphlets that tell users all about tick-borne illnesses and the procedures for removing ticks and taking care of the illnesses. We will also include tick ID cards that identify the different types of ticks.

Throughout the semester, we worked on our slogan, ingredients, sales, target market, and so much more. We got a long way, and reached our goals, goals such as getting our product in the store, making our first sale, making the bottles, presenting our product to real users, and more! Our slogan is: *Through Summer, Spring, and Fall, this spray stops them all!* Yes, maybe some slogans are better than ours, but it is the right slogan for our product!

The hardest part about making our product is understanding it takes time, but working on this project makes us happy. The happiness comes from our story—the story that starts with helping someone we care about and ends with making a difference. We have accomplished a lot this semester. We grew, we learned, we experienced, and we made our product: The Simple Spray!

———

Squirmy Virmies

In the first week of school, Andrew, Trent, and Logan were given the opportunity to select a project to work on for the first half of the school year. Our group decided to work on the Vermicomposting aspect of FH Grows.

First, we obtained two worm bins for our worms to live in. One was commercially made, and the other was homemade out of a rubber bin. Next, we prepared bedding for the apartments. Our bedding consisted of a moist mix of coco coir, newspaper, and cardboard. We then got leftover food from lunches that included fruits, vegetables, and bread or the worms to eat. We were able to set up the apartments for them the day before the 3,000 worms Mr. Aviles ordered arrived.

After the worms were put into their apartment and given food, the apartments were moved outside to our greenhouse. With this move to the greenhouse and the food in the bin, we were surprised plants began to grow in the worm apartments. Initially, we saw this as a major problem. For the first of two times, we contacted support at Uncle Jim's Worm Farm, where we bought the worms and spoke with Hannah. She told us that these plants were a natural aspect of worm bins that occurs, and it was nothing to worry about. She said tomatoes were particularly prone to growing in worm bins, which is what we had first fed the worms. With this knowledge, we thanked Hannah. Throughout the semester, we were continuously finding the plants growing in the worm bin, although now we knew that it was okay.

Week three was a learning curve for our group. By then, the worms finished their first round of food, and we were able to feed them again. We found that they really got comfortable in their bin. We saw that they were continuously eating their food, and we observed that they were really beginning to enjoy their stay. Throughout the first three weeks, we really got used to having them, and we learned to be responsible with them and knew what we had to do and got it done each week.

Sister Mushrooms

We wanted to share the challenges and successes of growing mushrooms. First, we need to start by introducing ourselves. We are the Sister Mushrooms. We are three seventh-grade girls wanting to learn how to grow the strange and mysterious white button mushrooms. It all started when we first walked into class on the first day of school, and Mr. Aviles had a list of things that he challenged us to try in the class. As we thought about taking on one of his challenges, we started to lean towards growing mushrooms. Even though none of us liked, or even ate mushrooms, we still were interested in how they were grown because the process was MUCH different than how you grow any other plant.

We decided to grow them and started researching how to grow mushrooms. To be honest, it started off rough because the requirements were a little out of the ordinary. It needed warm and humid temperature, as well as total darkness. We had to somehow mimic that. The closest thing we had to the warm woods mushrooms were found in was an empty cabinet in our recording studio. After knowing where to keep the mushrooms, we ordered a mushroom kit. The kit came, and we followed the instructions. After completing all the steps of the kit, we just had to wait, and wait, and wait.

After several weeks of nothing, we began to get worried about the health of the mushroom spores. Therefore, we went right back to the web to see why they might not be growing. After even more research, we turned to Mr. Aviles for help. He mentioned the idea that maybe some type of humidity tent to trap the warmth and moisture might help. As a result, we decided to dampen an old t-shirt and place that on top of the box.

We were amazed to come in, two days later, and find one giant mushroom. There was nothing but spores two days before. I believe that was when we got more into growing mushrooms. In the end, we got a great harvest from the kit. One week after the giant mushroom sprouted, we grew two pounds of white button mushrooms. Then, sadly, after we had cut and harvested the second batch of mushrooms, the whole box started to turn brown and die. Therefore, Mr. Aviles wanted to make a farm that would last much longer than the first box and to produce much more mushrooms. This is what we have been working on most of this semester: instead of buying a kit, we've made our own mushroom farm!

Our goal with the mushroom farm is to be the number one producer of mushrooms for our town pizza place, Umberto's. Before we even ordered the mushroom supplies, we sealed our deal with Umberto's. They agreed to buy all the mushrooms we could grow. As of this writing, we are waiting for our mushrooms to grow on the farm. We don't have mushrooms yet, but the spores look great!

We learned a lot in FH Grows. There were times when we got off track, and our mushrooms suffered. But we finally got our heads straight, and the mushrooms recovered. That's because we learned to take responsibility for something other than ourselves. We had to learn to work harder and if something were to go wrong, not to complain or give up. Because, again, we must take responsibility for our actions.

In the end, we believe that this business will go very far. We have plans to take this business to the next level by making it something kids can always do in FH Grows. There are many reasons to keep this project alive for as many years as there is FH Grows at Knollwood School: this mushroom project teaches kids how to take responsibility, pay attention, and care about things more than themselves.

———

Hydroponics Team

Our team is made up of Annie, Sofia, and Milana. Our project is hydroponics. What this means is we grow plants in water rather than soil. This process has benefits such as being able to grow anywhere because you can grow them indoors, and you don't need the sun; you can just use lights. Hydroponics also takes up much less space for growing than soil does.

Our goal was to sell our hydroponic basil to a local restaurant in town. We completed our goal by selling basil and other herbs to Umberto's, our local pizza place, every week. When you package the basil, you want to make sure that the basil has a little bit of stem left on so it can live longer. When we put the basil into the bag to give to Umberto's, we wanted to make sure we didn't squish the basil. Before we sold the basil, we weighed it. Finally, we brought the basil to our school office, and Umberto's picked it up. We loved seeing something that we grew and worked hard on in a local restaurant where other people can enjoy it.

We faced many problems with the hydroponics rack. We had an issue with our lights not turning on and flickering. This was an issue because the plants wouldn't be able to grow if we didn't have lights because they act as the sun when you grow indoors. We solved this problem by using pliers and adjusting the plug so the wires would fit properly. Next, thanks to a plant professional from Rutgers, we learned how our plants were too leggy (which means they weren't getting enough light), and we needed to make a way to move the lights up and down as the plant grew. Luckily, we solved our problem by creating a pulley system that we could use to adjust the distance of our lights from the plants.

———

Nicholas Creamery

As eighth-graders at Knollwood School, we have learned business and marketing skills that college students would learn. At the beginning of the first marking period, Mr. Aviles gave us the opportunity to create or grow a business. We chose to grow one, so we worked with Nicholas Creamery. Nicholas Creamery is a homemade, all-natural, small-batch ice cream shop located in Fair Haven and Atlantic Highlands.

For the past two marking periods, we have partnered with Nicholas Creamery. Mrs. Edwards, the owner of Nicholas Creamery, proposed the Peninsula Ice Cream war. The objective of this project was to advertise the business throughout schools in Monmouth county.

During the Peninsula Ice Cream war, six schools created a flavor and named it based off of their school. We advised each school to make more than one flavor, if Nicholas Creamery's ice cream maker could not make one of the flavors. After each school submitted both of its flavors, Nicholas Creamery made the flavors and sold them from March 1st to March 31st. The school with the most sales received 10% of the profit and an ice cream social for its school.

Not only did we help organize the ice cream war for the county, but we also organized the contest within our school, too. To come up with a flavor for our school, we made a series of Google Forms with the help of our principal, Mrs. Romano. In the first form, we asked that each student in our school come up with their own ice cream flavor and a name. We also advised each student to be as creative as possible. For the first Google Form, we made three different forms: one for fourth grade, one for fifth grade, and one for all of the sixth, seventh, and eighth grades. Once a majority of the students submitted a flavor, we narrowed them down to five per grade and made a new form with the five flavors. In this form, all students voted on which one out of the five from their grade they would want as our school's flavor. In the third form, we took the most popular flavor from each of the three forms and made one last form to send out to all of the students in the school. With this form, we found out the top flavor for our school.

By doing this project, we learned many skills most schools don't offer to their students. Mr. Aviles's goal for the eighth grade was to introduce us to real-life business situations. From this project, we got the opportunity to do just that. We saw how a small project such as an ice cream contest could benefit a local business. We now have experience in this type of work, which will help us in the future. After the semester is over, another group of eighth-graders at Knollwood will take over the business and continue to work with Nicholas Creamery. In the future, we hope that this project will help to grow Nicholas Creamery and gain them more business. We are very thankful for this opportunity and all of the knowledge we obtained.

———

Student Lawn and Dog Care

We are Student Lawn and Dog Care, a student-run lawn care business. That means that we are working on trying and helping out the people in town that don't have the time or energy to rake their leaves, mow their lawn, walk their dog, or shovel their snow. We have also made a commitment to help out the elderly and take time out of our day to make sure their leaves and snow are taken care of.

In the beginning, we focused on getting our name out there as a student-run business. We wanted to make sure people knew they could trust us and our work. We live close to most of our customers, so it is important that they know we will do a good job and hopefully recommend us to others.

Outside of class, we handed out at least 600 fliers listing our services and contact information. During this class period, Mr. Aviles taught us the importance of marketing and making the best of the time that we have by planning "next steps." He helped us learn to give pitches and helped us not be nervous to talk to people. He has also taught us how to grow our business via social media marketing and be strategic when handing out flyers around town by tracking what streets we had advertised on and how many customers we got from that street. He also helped us advertise using the FH Leads Facebook page, with over 600 followers, to help spread the word to local parents.

All this marketing and planning eventually led to us receiving emails and messages from people in town. We got a lot of jobs, and we wound up making over $1500.

As we made money, we bought things that would help your business grow. We bought a leaf-blower and rakes as well as wristbands and t-shirts to help us advertise. We had fun running our business, which we plan to have for a long time.

————

The Wash House

FH Leads is a program in the school where we eighth graders help to grow the small businesses in our town, while also learning the ins and outs of owning a small business and working with others. At the beginning of the year, we were assigned to work with the Wash House. This is a laundromat in town that is run by a mother and a daughter, Geri and Geri. This family business started in 1998. The Wash House has a wide variety of customers. When we met with them at first, they told us that their customer base was mainly Latinx. They said that this could be difficult at times, given the language barrier, but they ultimately love their business. Their small business also has lots of washing machines and dryers. Also, they are a wash-dry-fold, so the employees will also fold and organize the customers' clothes for them. In terms of location, the Wash House is located in a tough-to-find place: it is in the back of a shopping center where you must know about it to go there. For example, people from out of town might be driving by and not even notice it. However, with recent renovations to the shopping center, the Wash House now has a sign in front and looks more appealing from the visible portion of the street.

As we talked with the Wash House more, we learned that their main needs and concerns were that they needed a new Point-of-Sale (POS) System. We began by researching what a POS System actually was. After our research, we learned that it was a system that helps the process of payment between the customer and the cashier/employee. We also learned that the functionality of different POS Systems ranges from remembering customers to understanding multiple languages, to self-check-out for the customer. Now that we knew what the POS System was and what it functioned for, we began our quest to find the best one for the Wash House. To do this, we started by looking at what other laundromats had done all over the country. This research taught us that many options worked for many different types of businesses and laundromats. This made us think that the best option would be to choose a variety of quality POS systems and present what they can do for the Wash House. After hours of researching through many class periods, we finally compiled all of our information to find the three best options for the Wash House.

After this, the Wash House got back to us, and they let us know that they loved what we gave them. Not only did we give them various options, but we also provided the precise information they needed on each system. They then told us that they would let us know when they made their final decision on which system they would pick that we suggested for them. A few weeks later, they let us know what they decided.

This was almost the ending point of our work with the Wash House. With our main mission completed, we thought that we could do a little more. Thus, we went on to help them out in a few other ways. To start, we made a customer satisfaction survey to gather feedback and customers' demographics and satisfaction rate. We then made them an ad that is versatile for both social media or a physical advertisement. Finally, we attempted to remove bad and unreasonable reviews on the Internet about the Wash House and added positive ones we got from customers.

Ultimately, this work with the POS System and the other work made us appreciate the Wash House and what it is like to own a small business. Not only is it a great business, but the owners who we collaborated with were hard workers, kind, and completely dedicated to the betterment of their small business. As much as we loved working with them, they also loved working with us. Therefore, they added a portion to their website dedicated to the program and students at Knollwood School. This illustrates the great importance of what we did this year. We not only helped a small business, but we got closer to the people in our community!

———

Luck for Pups

Our business, Luck for Pups, started two years ago. It all happened when our teacher, Mr. Aviles, challenged us to start a business that made a product that improved the world. We chose to help animals, of course!

We wanted to help improve both the lives of dogs in shelters and dogs bored at home. We went for a trip to our local ASPCA to see what it was like to be a shelter dog, probably the most bored dogs in the world. We learned that they only left their cage a few hours a day. Otherwise, they were in their cage. Most dogs had toys like tennis balls in their cage, but no one to throw it to them, so we knew we had to make a toy that a dog could play with by itself and would stimulate its mind.

Our toy is a cylinder tube with a screw-on lid and holes all around the body. The way our toy works is very simple. First, you take off the screw-on lid and load in your dog's favorite treats. Then you just screw the lid right back on. Throughout the day, your dog will roll the toy around, and for all the hard work, a treat will appear at random. As a result, the dog will not be bored, and you will not have to feel bad, leaving the dog at home all day.

Another great thing about our toy is that it has a random reward schedule. That means there is not a pattern for when the treats come out or what hole they come out of. We did this because we learned that random rewards, things like slot machines, are very engaging and motivating for the user.

To help tell people about our toy, we created an Instagram account to advertise our business. We started off by reaching out to popular dog accounts and asked them to send us pictures to use on our Instagram and also to give us shoutouts on their Instagram. We made our Instagram unique and part of our brand by making a theme. We did this by using dog quotes in between each picture of a dog. Our Instagram uses the same colors, from our brand, and keeps the same fonts. We constantly update our Instagram (you can follow it @luck.for.pups), and we have over 50 posts right now. We also post a lot on our Instagram Story, where we ask our followers what they think about our toy, such as, what they think the name should be and if they would be interested in trying our toy out. Also, we work hard to produce more content for our growing 150 followers.

We also researched a lot about hashtags to use for social media marketing. We found hashtags that relate to our pictures, and can bring in new followers who like posts that use those hashtags. We put many hashtags in our posts to try to get our page to grow. Also, we linked to our GoFundMe in our Instagram bio, so when people visit our page, they can donate to it if they want to since making a dog toy is really expensive.

After getting our name out there, we started working on turning our prototype into a real dog toy by talking to manufacturers and getting quotes from different toy companies. We got quotes for our packaging, too. We had to research the best type of material to use for our packaging and our toy and make sure both were safe for dogs. We talked with a few manufacturers, but so far, the one who gave us the lowest price was a manufacturer who specializes in rapid prototyping.

When we first talked to the rapid prototyping company, we were instructed to send over CAD files so they could give us an estimate. We didn't know how to make CAD files, so Mr. Aviles suggested we email our high school's CAD teacher and see if he or his students could turn our dog toy into a CAD file, so we did. After waiting a few days, we had our CAD file! This helped us a lot because we were able to get an accurate quote. We have also spoken to a lot of representatives at the manufacturer to make sure the rubber was safe for dogs and to check shipping costs.

We are still working on our dog toy even though our time in FH Leads is almost over. As class comes to an end, we plan to continue our business by updating our Instagram posts, getting the toy made, and contacting lots of customers who may want to try our toy. The most exciting news is that Kong saw our social media posts and are interested in helping us make our toy. Who knows what will happen next?

———

Teacher: Mark Suter
EdCorps: Grit 9 Design
School: Elidia High School
Location: Elida, Ohio
Grade/Subject: Technology

It All Started When…
I grew up with my family's retail produce operation, Suter's Produce. As a result, I've been working side-by-side with high school students since I was driving tractors at seven-years-old. The game-changer was my dad teaching more than just picking sweetcorn—he invested in the kids.

Those summers, along with the unconventional junior high teaching methods of my grandmother Wauneta, are the greatest influences on my approach to teaching: It's about the students, not the tests.

Beginning in 2009, I grew so tired of planned curriculum that I began asking students questions like, "You did the web design assignment, but how would you fare with a client sitting here right beside you? What would you say? How do you track what you've done? What about costs?" And so, the Ridgemont Tech Club, aka "Gopher Nation," was born—creating ugly websites and even worse video production. We were terrible...at first, and we openly talked about our terribleness, and what we had to do to get better. We once took an industrial stage lighting rig with can lights to an on-location video shoot, casting huge shadows on the wall behind the subject...and thought we were awesome. And to think, my tech club president then, Joe Capehart, was just offered a job at Vimeo (web video company) in New York City. I can't take credit, but I'll take influence. Now in my third year at Elida High School in 2018, I think back to day one. I told myself, "I'm new here, I'll wait a semester or even a year to get to know the kids before starting an EdCorp." I made it EIGHT DAYS before I invited a slew of students to a meeting where I told them, "I'd like to invite you to be part of a new family, a new team that will run a business right here in this classroom. There are no assignments or tests, and I have no idea if this will work, but I'm willing to try if you are. What do you say?" Grit9 was born.

I still feel like I'm doing a horrible job, and I struggle with keeping up with web design platforms and ramping up individual students' confidence to take over client meetings, phone calls, and emails. I openly share my anxieties with my team and ask for their help. I'm not pretending to need help as a trick to get them to do work; this actually falls apart without them. Paperwork? Don't even start, I'm a hot mess. I tell my treasurer, "Can you keep track of all of this and keep our district treasurer informed, cause I can't?" And so, she does, thankfully. This same level of expectation and trust is given to everyone on the team, unless they do something that compromises that trust. My open vulnerability elicits their own, and the fragile seed of trust grows into a mighty oak. Ok, that's cliché, and it doesn't always go like that. I just know that this approach has fruited a more positive influence on students than when my classroom was boring, when I tried to manufacture artificial fun, but everything still smelled like school.

"Smells Like School..."

Kids are smart. They have a nose for so-called "fun" activities that, in reality, still feel like they are at school. Those are activities that "smell like [traditional] school." In my classroom, every activity I do, I give it the smell-test. Here's a breakdown:

Smells like school:

- Simulations, worksheets, textbooks.
- Problems are CLEAR and given. Teacher holds the answer.
- Activities are in the comfort zone of the teacher.
- Students are looking for which hoop to jump through to get the grade they desire and move on.
- Mistakes are giggled at and ridiculed, lowering the positivity and trust level.
- Students are individuals who work in groups...if they have to.
- There is a sense of calm, sometimes bordering boredom...on both sides (students and teachers).

Refreshing scents of real life:

- A sense of excitement, sometimes bordering on chaos...from students and teacher.
- Problems are initially messy, and difficult to separate into cleaner, bite-size problems. Teacher doesn't always know the answer either.
- Students have overlapping shared goals and willingly consult/assist impromptively.
- Simulations only exist in preparation for a real, student-guided event.
- Mistakes as a result of risk-taking are reframed as a source of pride and progress, showing mutual trust, strengthening the classroom's culture.
- Teacher. Models. Desired. Behaviors. (Screw up. Share it. Adjust it. Twist it. Bop it.)
- Activities are out of the comfort zone...for students AND teacher.

So how do you integrate an EdCorp into your classroom?

Step One: Build trust.

My wife and I were once on a getaway in Milwaukee, WI, and upon attempting to check in for our flight home, we were appalled to find out our airline WENT OUT OF BUSINESS. Gone. No planes, ever. We watched as others approached kiosks and discovered the same problem. How will we get home to Columbus, OH? *Lightbulb.* Problem: Many of us need to get to Columbus. Solution: "Hey! Uh, anyone want to rent a van and share driving to get us to Columbus?"
As we rolled into Columbus the next day like Muppets in The Electric Mayhem bus, it was a bittersweet ending to the camaraderie that developed with our van load of passengers. Humans that endure shared adversity together grow closer.

As a teacher, I need to be feeling some authentic discomfort if I ever expect my students to do the same. I frequently find myself saying things like, "You guys, I'll be honest, I'm hesitating to dial this number because I have anxiety about what they will say, and will I have the right answers." This is not just being out of my comfort zone; it's fully disclosing it as well. Students may think we have it all together, which is intimidating if they feel like they do not.

Ok, we built trust. Now what?

Step Two: Build "The Master Plan" by asking the right questions.
An EdCorp needs a plan that guides all decision making. A method that has exploded in popularity is the "Business Model Canvas" (BMC). It's what our business, Grit9 (grit9.com), uses. In our classroom, it's a giant sheet of craft paper we draw black lines to divide it into the boxes that follow the template design. There are some nice animated explanations of BMC on YouTube by Strategyzer. I print out blank BMC templates and have each student fill in each box as I describe what it's asking for. Then we debate answers and

write the final one up on the giant craft paper. It gets us asking questions like, "Who is our target audience? What makes our product/service better than our competition?" and so on.

(Pro-tip: If you don't have a product/service yet, you can scour Etsy.com for ideas, or look at what other EdCorps are doing)

Step Three: Find someone smarter to answer those questions.

My dad tells this true story where a guy comes to the farm and describes his plan in detail of how he's going to start a produce business like our farm Suter's Produce (see suterproduce.com), including what varieties he'll plant and what his costs will be. He then gets back in his truck and drives away. Dad then asks whomever he's telling the story to, "What did this guy do wrong?" He goes on to explain—the guy who's never farmed did not ask ANY questions from the guy that's been doing it his whole life. He just decided to make a "plan" and took off.

The moral is, you don't HAVE to know how to run a business, market a product, budget finances, or manage employees. You just need to get your students courageous enough to ask someone who can. They know they may be rejected; that's a risk they will only take if comfortable with their peers and the teacher. That's why you started with trust.

As for how to find those people with answers, there's a go-to method we use at Grit9:

Call your local Chamber of Commerce and explain your question, ask who you can talk to about it. This has led to many opportunities for my students to speak at chamber events in front of lots of business owners (who coincidentally need new websites that we just so happen to make), building their own individual brand, confidence, and resumes.

"My students are hesitant to take these risks, how do I get them going?"

Step Four: Be a Super Blooper Model

Before expecting your students to find these people, model what it looks like yourself first under the condition that they will be taking over next time. It IS nerve-wracking putting yourself on speakerphone and cold-calling someone for help, and the students will feel better about their own anxiety towards it if they see you showing the same symptoms. Go out of your way to show vulnerability; it's where the smell of school dissipates.

MARK'S STORY captures what makes entrepreneurship in the classroom so special. As teachers, we are always looking for better ways to get our kids to fall in love with learning. As a teacher looking for a better way to engage his students, like me, Mark turned to entrepreneurship. Like most entrepreneurs, Mark doesn't have a formal business background, but what Mark does have is the mindset it takes to be an entrepreneur. Mark is excited, motivated, resourceful, and knows that there is always more to learn.

By having the right mindset, Mark became the COO of his classroom. Through entrepreneurship, Mark is modeling and helping students grow that same mindset. Mark and his students are courageous to do some silo-busting through their EdCorp even though they aren't experts yet. They take their best guesses, learn from their mistakes, and always keep moving forward.

That's the beauty of entrepreneurship. It's a mirror. Even if Mark's students never go on to be entrepreneurs, the mindset they develop and the skills they will grow trying to start a successful business can be used anywhere students find themselves after they graduate. That is because what they have put into their business, they are going to get out of it. The real, relevant learning found in running an EdCorp gives students the most valuable lesson of all, real-world experience.

Chapter 7

RESOURCES

bit.ly/edcorpsclassroomrescources

This is a QR code for all of the resources discussed in the book. The resources used in my program are constantly changing, so having a Google folder where you can get the most updated resources will make sure you have all the latest tools you'll need to run your EdCorp.

NOTES

4. Silo Busting with Key Activities

1. Dam, Rikke, and Teo Siang. "Stage 2 in the Design Thinking Process: Define the Problem and Interpret the Results." *The Interaction Design Foundation*, https://www.interaction-design.org/literature/article/stage-2-in-the-design-thinking-process-define-the-problem-and-interpret-the-results.
2. Sinek, Simon. "How Great Leaders Inspire Action." *TED*, https://www.ted.com/talks/simon_sinek_how_great_leaders_inspire_action.
3. Lake, Laura. "An Overview of Brand Identity and Steps to Defining Your Brand." *The Balance Small Business*, The Balance Small Business, 10 Jan. 2019, https://www.thebalancesmb.com/define-your-brand-identity-2294834.

ABOUT THE AUTHOR

Chris Aviles is a teacher at Knollwood middle school in the Fair Haven school district in Fair Haven, New Jersey. There he runs the renown Fair Haven Innovates program he created in 2015. Chris is passionate about entrepreneurship in the classroom because he has seen the amazing things that can happen when you make learning real and relevant through student-run businesses. Chris is considered an expert in Entrepreneurship, Gamification, Game-Based Learning, Passion Projects, Project-Based Learning, School Gardens, Blended Learning, and Makerspaces. He is a Google Certified Innovator, Trainer, and GEG Leader. Chris is also a Raspberry Pi Certified Educator, Microsoft Innovative Educator, and has a Masters in Educational Technology. You can keep up with Chris on his blog Teched Up Teacher.

OTHER EDUMATCH TITLES

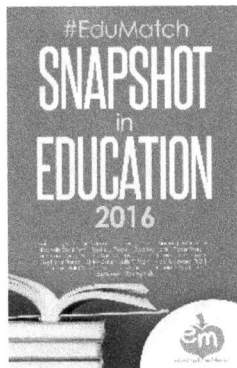

EduMatch Snapshot in Education (2016)
In this collaborative project, twenty educators located throughout the
United States share educational strategies that have worked well for
them, both with students and in their professional practice.

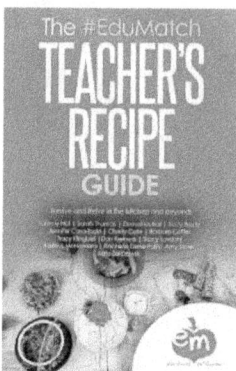

The #EduMatch Teacher's Recipe Guide
Editors: Tammy Neil & Sarah Thomas
Dive in as fourteen international educators share their recipes for
success, both literally and metaphorically!

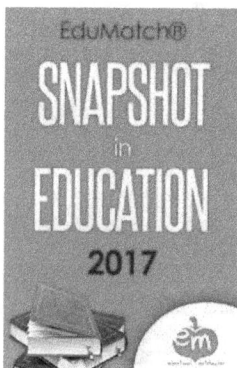

EduMatch Snapshot in Education (2017)
We're back! EduMatch proudly presents Snapshot in Education (2017).
In this two-volume collection, 32 educators and one student share their
tips for the classroom and professional practice.

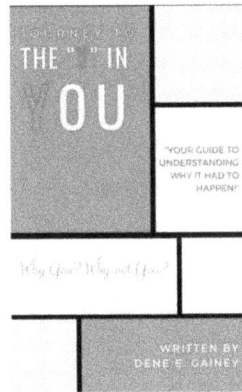

Journey to The "Y" in You by Dene Gainey
This book started as a series of separate writing pieces that were eventually woven together to form a fabric called The Y in You. The question is, "What's the 'why' in you?"

The Teacher's Journey by Brian Costello
Follow the Teacher's Journey with Brian as he weaves together the stories of seven incredible educators. Each step encourages educators at any level to reflect, grow, and connect.

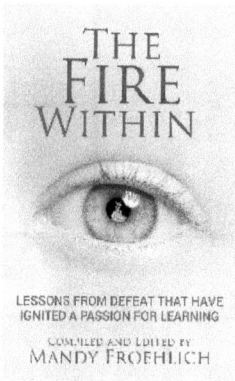

THE FIRE WITHIN

LESSONS FROM DEFEAT THAT HAVE
IGNITED A PASSION FOR LEARNING

COMPILED AND EDITED BY
MANDY FROEHLICH

The Fire Within
Compiled and edited by Mandy Froehlich
Adversity itself is not what defines us. It is how we react to that adversity and the choices we make that creates who we are and how we will persevere.

EduMagic by Sam Fecich
This book challenges the thought that "teaching" begins only after certification and college graduation. Instead, it describes how students in teacher preparation programs have value to offer their future colleagues, even as they are learning to be teachers!

Makers in Schools
Editors: Susan Brown & Barbara Liedahl
*The maker mindset sets the stage for the Fourth Industrial Revolution,
empowering educators to guide their students.*

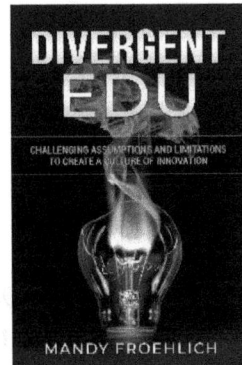

Divergent EDU by Mandy Froehlich
*The concept of being innovative can be made to sound so simple. But
what if the development of the innovative thinking isn't the only
roadblock?*

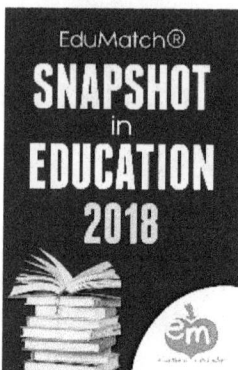

EduMatch Snapshot in Education (2018)
EduMatch® is back for our third annual Snapshot in Education. Dive in as 21 educators share a snapshot of what they learned, what they did, and how they grew in 2018.

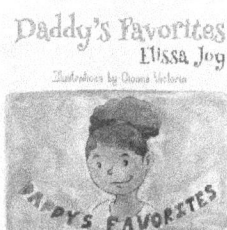

Daddy's Favorites by Elissa Joy
Illustrated by Dionne Victoria
Five-year-old Jill wants to be the center of everyone's world. But, her most favorite person in the world, without fail, is her Daddy. But Daddy has to be Daddy, and most times that means he has to be there when everyone needs him, especially when her brother Danny needs him.

Level Up Leadership by Brian Kulak
Gaming has captivated its players for generations and cemented itself as a fundamental part of our culture. In order to reach the end of the game, they all need to level up.

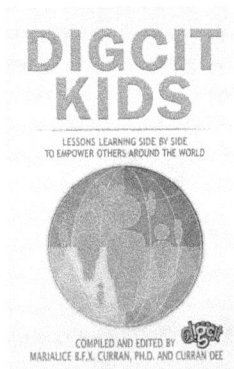

DigCit Kids edited by Marialice Curran & Curran Dee
This book is a compilation of stories, starting with our own mother and son story, and shares examples from both parents and educators on how they embed digital citizenship at home and in the classroom.

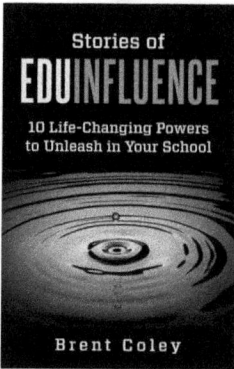

Stories of EduInfluence by Brent Coley
In Stories of EduInfluence, veteran educator Brent Coley shares stories from more than two decades in the classroom and front office.

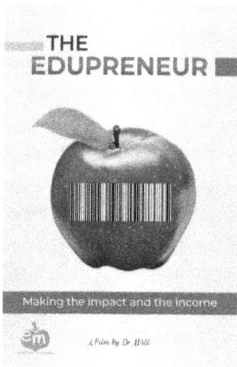

The Edupreneur by Dr. Will
The Edupreneur is a 2019 documentary film that takes you on a journey into the successes and challenges of some of the most recognized names in K-12 education consulting.

In Other Words by Rachelle Dene Poth
In Other Words is a book full of inspirational and thought-provoking quotes that have pushed the author's thinking and inspired her.

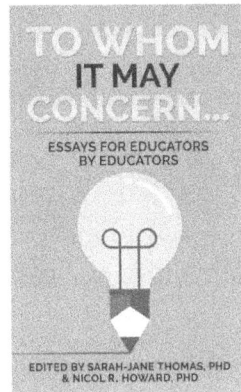

To Whom it May Concern
Editors: Sarah-Jane Thomas, PhD & Nicol R. Howard, PhD
In *To Whom it May Concern...*, you will read a collaboration between two Master's in Education classes at two universities on opposite coasts of the United States.

One Drop of Kindness by Jeff Kubiak
This children's book, along with each of you, will change our world as we know it. It only takes *One Drop of Kindness to fill a heart with love.*

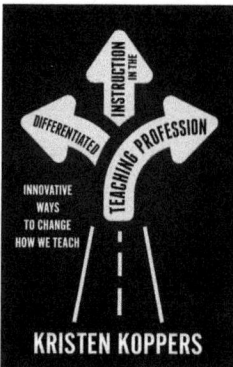

Differentiated Instruction in the Teaching Profession by Kristen Koppers
Differentiated Instruction in the Teaching Profession is an innovative way to use critical thinking skills to create strategies to help all students succeed. This book is for educators of all levels who want to take the next step into differentiating their instruction.

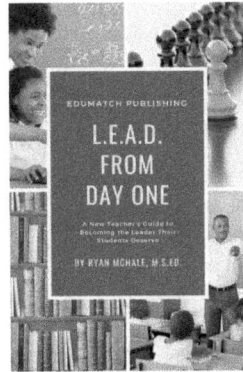

L.E.A.D. from Day One by Ryan McHale
L.E.A.D. from Day One is a go-to resource to help educators outline a future plan toward becoming a teacher leader. The purpose of this book is to help you see just how easily you can transform your entire mindset to become the leader your students need you to be.

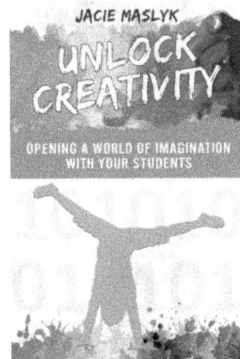

Unlock Creativity by Jacie Maslyk
Every classroom is filled with creative potential. *Unlock Creativity* will help you discover opportunities that will make every student see themselves as a creative thinker.

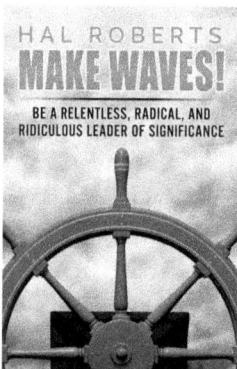

Make Waves! by Hal Roberts

In *Make Waves!* Hal discusses 15 attributes of a great leader. He shares his varied experience as a teacher, leader, a player in the N.F.L., and a plethora of research to take you on a journey to emerge as leader of significance.

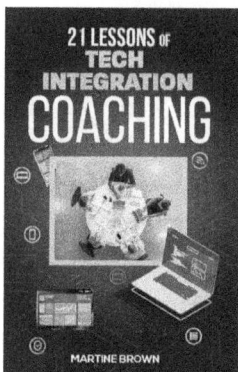

21 Lessons of Tech Integration Coaching by Martine Brown

In *21 Lessons of Tech Integration Coaching*, Martine Brown provides a practical guide about how to use your skills to support and transform schools.

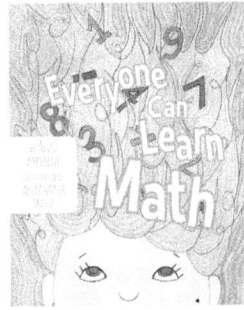

Everyone Can Learn Math by Alice Aspinall
How do you approach a math problem that challenges you? Do you keep trying until you reach a solution? Or are you like Amy, who gets frustrated easily and gives up?

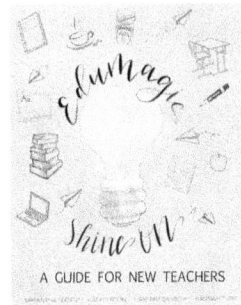

EduMagic Shine On by Sam Fecich, Katy Gibson, Hannah Sansom, and Hannah Turk
EduMagic: A Guide for New Teachers picks up where *EduMagic: A Guide for Preservice Teachers* leaves off. Dr. Sam Fecich is back at the coffee shop and is now joined by three former students-turned-friends. She is excited to introduce you to these three young teachers: Katy Gibson, Hannah Sansom, and Hannah Turk.

All In by Kristen Nan & Jacie Maslyk

Unlike Nevada's slogan of "what happens in Vegas, stays in Vegas," this book reminds us that what happens in the classroom, should never stay within the classroom! It spotlights a unique relationship between a forward-thinking teacher and a future-focused district administrator.

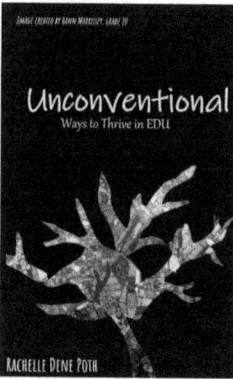

Unconventional by Rachelle Dene Poth

Unconventional will empower educators to take risks, explore new ideas and emerging technologies, and bring amazing changes to classrooms. Dive in to transform student learning and thrive in edu!

EduMatch Publishing

www.ingramcontent.com/pod-product-compliance
Lightning Source LLC
Chambersburg PA
CBHW071421210326
41597CB00020B/3598